EDMUND BURKE
and HIS WORLD

ALSO BY ALICE P. MILLER

Books for Young Readers:

THE HEART OF CAMP WHIPPOORWILL
THE LITTLE STORE ON THE CORNER
MAKE WAY FOR PEGGY O'OBRIEN!

Others:

THE 1910-1919 DECADE

EDMUND BURKE
and HIS WORLD

Alice P. Miller

Introduction by RUSSELL KIRK

With Illustrations

The Devin-Adair Company
Old Greenwich

In memory of my mother

Julia A. McCarthy

native of Bandon, County Cork

and

long-time resident of the

rebellious Commonwealth of Massachusetts

Acknowledgments

I cannot, like Dr. Johnson in his famous letter to Lord Chesterfield, claim that I wrote this book "with so little obligation to any favourer of learning." Many "favourers of learning" have had a hand in creating it. No patron helped to finance the research, but I did get help from many persons with special qualifications.

First, I want to thank librarians and museum curators in the United States, England, and Ireland for their efficiency, courtesy, and enthusiasm. They made it easier for me to spend my reasearch time more profitably. Most of the material I needed for this book was available at the New York Public Library. But certain little touches that add sparkle to the text were often found in other places — the library of the Cherwell Center in Oxford, England, for example, or the library of Trinity College in Dublin, Ireland. Browsing in secondhand bookstores here and there also resulted in the discovery of certain interesting material that might not have been readily located in any library catalogue.

Several other persons spent hours reading some portion of the text or even a long draft. Archbishop Fulton J. Sheen read one long version of this book when he was over eighty and when he must have had many other demands on his time. He was generous enough to send me a letter indicating that he had read the text carefully and appreciatively. A portion of that letter states: "Long before there was any mention of 'civil rights,' Edmund Burke had dedicated his life to that noble cause." Father Theodore M. Hesburgh, President of the University of Notre Dame, also sent me a warmly appreciative letter.

The Reverend Dr. Pauli Murray, the first black woman to be ordained an Episcopalian priest, read the text with special attention and sent me a long letter about it. Since she had a brilliant career as a lawyer before she entered a theological seminary, she was particularly interested in Burke's concern with legislation relating to civil rights. "One thing the book did for me," she said, "was to give me a more balanced view of Burke; my general impression was that he was an arch-conservative. Your portrait of his concern for the rights of Americans, Roman Catholics, and the people of India gave me new insights." She also told me that one of the few books she has from her father's library is "a small volume published in 1893 and entitled *Selections from the Speeches and Writings of Edmund Burke.* One or two passages were underlined, e.g., an excerpt on 'Ambition.' " Her father was a principal in a public school in Baltimore at a time when the speeches of Burke formed an important part of the curriculum.

Others who have been in some significant way helpful in creating this book are Elizabeth Hodges, writer and librarian; Gertrude Hecker Winders, author of juvenile biographies; editors Frances Keene, Donna Brooks, Margaret Adams, and Florence Norton; Dr. Blanche Blank, Vice-President of Yeshiva University; and Dr. Riley Hughes, professor of English at Georgetown University. These persons vary considerably in age, religion, ethnic background, and specialties, Their comments and their questions have been of incalculable value in showing me how to make the life of a complex man understandable to the general reader. And that is important, for this book is intended for the general reader rather than for the specialist.

To members of my family I owe a debt that can probably be appreciated only by families who have had to put up with the presence of a writer in the household. It must have been bewildering at times to my daughters Nancy and Jacqueline to have a mother "living" in the eighteenth century and carrying on an affair with Oliver Goldsmith, my favorite character in this story. Since my daughters were attending college while I was doing research for this book, they sometimes brought me material from their college libraries.

My husband, Warren Hudson Miller, has helped in more ways and over a longer period of time than anyone else. I would have dedicated this book to him had it not seemed more appropriate to dedicate it to my Irish-born mother. Were it not for her, I might never have acquired the skills needed to write such a book.

CONTENTS

Introduction

According to a modern German scholar, Hans Barth, the most important political thinker of recent centuries is Edmund Burke; for Burke, more than anyone else, understood that social order depends upon a healthy tension between the claims of order and the claims of freedom. Burke was a practical politician, and yet far more than a practical politician.

Also Edmund Burke was a courageous, honest, and attractive man. Alice P. Miller presents a lively and moving portrait of him — the more valuable because the details of his life have been difficult to patch together, since Burke himself, always immensely busy with public affairs, gives us few details about his personal existence in the nine big volumes of his correspondence. This book will be valuable to both adults and to the rising generation of the last quarter of this turbulent twentieth century.

Even in his college days Burke foresaw that the world was entering upon a time of terrible troubles. He fought magnificently against disorder — in England, in Ireland, in India, in America, in the European continent. He looms so large that, as Woodrow Wilson wrote, we sense no incongruity when we speak of "Edmund Burke and the French Revolution." His writings and speeches are grander than all the tracts and pamphlets of the Revolutionaries combined.

Yet there exists, strangely enough, no standard edition of Burke's work. For many people, Mrs. Miller's good book will be their first introduction not only to Burke's thought, but to the personality of the man. Some of his sentences and some of his actions may influence such readers for the rest of their lives.

Burke was a major political thinker (against his will, for he distrusted "political metaphysicians"); a grand master of English rhetoric; the principal architect of the first modern political party; a historian so important that Lord Acton declared that "history begins with Burke"; and a man whose character makes him an exemplar for anyone who even dabbles in public affairs. Also he was cheerful (most of the time), generous, and a wonderful talker. Mrs. Miller touches perceptively upon all these talents.

Edmund Burke even influenced the Constitution of the United States, though he never discussed that document, for Chief Justice John Marshall, who molded the Constitution into its enduring form, was Burke's disciple. His influence is growing in our time, as much scholarly publication about him in recent years suggests. Mrs. Miller, familiar with this recent scholarship, gives us in winning biographical form Burke's head and heart.

Once upon a time, nearly every secondary-school pupil in America was expected to read attentively Burke's speech on conciliation with the American colonies. (Nowadays such pupils are not expected to read any great orators.) *Edmund Burke and His World* will accomplish something to restore Americans' awareness of their inheritance from this warmhearted man of genius.

— RUSSELL KIRK

Mecosta, Michigan

1. The First Years
(1729-1744)

IN A TALL, narrow, steep-gabled house on the banks of the River Liffey in Dublin, Ireland, a brown-eyed boy was born on January 12, 1729. His father was a prosperous Protestant attorney. His mother was Catholic.

The fact that the father was a Protestant was important, very important. The Protestants and Catholics of Ireland lived in different worlds and were unlikely to meet in a way that would lead to marriage. When such marriages did occur, it was the custom for the children to be reared in the faith of the parent of the same sex. Thus the little brown-eyed boy, whose name was Edmund Burke, was brought up as a member of the Established Church, as were his two brothers, Garrett and Richard. He had only one sister who survived early childhood. Her name was Juliana, and she was a Catholic, like her mother.

Had Edmund Burke's father been a Catholic, he might never have learned to read and write. He might never have tasted a piece of bread and butter or slept in a shelter that offered ample protection against the wind and rain. For all that he was blessed with genius, he might never have developed his gifts in a country where genius was crippled if it happened to be bestowed on a Catholic.

The animosity between Irish Catholics and Irish Protestants continues to this day. It still destroys lives and brings heartbreak to the survivors. But the situation was different in the early eighteenth century. At that time the small island nation was not split into two even smaller nations. The Catholics, far more numerous than the Protestants, had no power. The Catholics were being punished because they had supported the Catholic King James II in his bid for the English throne. The Protestants supported King William. And it was the supporters of King William who won a victory at a battle fought on the banks of the River Boyne on July 12, 1690. Following that victory the English Protestant settlers in Ireland took the best land from the Catholics and passed laws designed to keep the Catholics too weak to rebel. Catholics were denied an education, they were not allowed to own property, they could not improve their lot by working hard. They lived in such misery that foreign visitors to Ireland found it almost incredible, even after they had seen that misery with their own eyes. A not untypical comment was one made by a Frenchman: "I have seen the Indian in his forest and the Negro in his chains and thought then that I had beheld the lowest term in human misery, but I did not know the lot of Ireland."

Little Ned Burke, snug in his comfortable home in one of the better residential neighborhoods of Dublin, knew nothing of that kind of misery during his childhood years. Indeed he knew little about the city of Dublin, for he lived there only a few years after his birth. Dublin was not a very healthful place for babies. Every spring the river overflowed its banks and epidemics spread through the city, taking the lives of many children. In one such epidemic little Ned became seriously ill. Although he survived, he was left with a limp that would make him walk awkwardly for the rest of his life. And he was so delicate that he was sent to County Cork in southern Ireland to live with his mother's Catholic relatives, the Nagles. (Ireland is as far north as Labrador, but its shores are washed by the Gulf Stream, and its southern counties have a temperate climate.)

Ned's father would never have sent him to live with Catholics had there been the slightest likelihood that they would try to convert the boy to their own faith. Ned's father wanted his sons to rise in the world. As Catholics, they would have been denied all opportunities. As members of the Established Church, they could enjoy an excellent education and live a rewarding life. Ned's Catholic relatives were to take good care of him and would be paid by being allowed to live in far greater comfort than most Catholics. Ned's father owned the land on which they lived; they did not, like most Catholics, need to fear that they might be evicted. Yet, if Ned was not exposed to Catholic doctrines, he did learn from his Catholic relatives that Catholics could be decent. He would never, like some Protestants, hate Catholics simply because they were Catholics.

He was a bright little boy, with red hair, brown eyes, and engaging freckles. And his limp didn't prevent him from running and playing on the large estate where the Nagles lived. The Nagle clan had at one time been one of Ireland's most distinguished families, and their land was extraordinarily beautiful. With its moss-covered ruins, dreamy mists, and summer twilights that lingered far into the night, it was like a setting for a fairy tale. It was in fact the very countryside that had inspired the poet Edmund Spenser — a distant relative of Ned's — while he was writing *The Faerie Queene*. Ned acquired a taste for old things that was to remain with him all his life. He loved old trees that had stood in the same spot for centuries. He loved buildings that had acquired long histories. He loved the legends of long ago that his Catholic relatives recited to him, legends in which minstrels sang ballads and played harps in the halls of the old Irish kings. Life was serene at Ballyduff, and his Catholic relatives lavished affection on him.

But he would not be allowed to spend many years in idle dreaming. Back in Dublin, his father was making ambitious plans for his sons. Their education must begin early. While

Ned was still a little lad, he went off to school each day in a crumbling castle on the Nagle estate. His teacher was a hedge-schoolmaster named O'Halloran.

Hedge-schoolmasters were so called because they gave lessons to Catholics in secret, usually behind hedges in the fields. Since Catholics were supposed to be kept in ignorance, the hedge-schoolmaster ran great risks in instructing them. If discovered, he could be sentenced to life imprisonment. But the hedge-schoolmaster continued to roam about the Irish countryside, an inkpot slung around his neck on a chain and books stashed in his shabby pockets, determined to keep the spark of learning alive among the Catholics. The hedge-schoolmaster was usually well versed in the Latin and Greek classics and a mathematician of no mean attainments. Since lessons might be interrupted at any moment, the pupils gulped down knowledge as fast as they could swallow it. Latin and Greek, geometry and logic were of no use in planting potatoes. They did keep minds from rusting. And a time might come when some of the pupils would themselves become hedge-schoolmasters and pass the torch of learning along to a new generation.

Since Catholics had no money to pay for their schooling, the hedge-schoolmaster did much of his work with no reward other than the satisfaction of knowing that he was helping his countrymen. But sometimes a hedge-schoolmaster might earn his room and board and a bit of cash by teaching Protestant boys, and O'Halloran was delighted at the opportunity to teach Ned and a few other boys from the neighborhood. They had no blackboards or desks or most of the other things that we associate with classrooms. But they did have paper and ink and books — and studying in a room of an old castle was pleasant. O'Halloran was a rousing good teacher, and Ned was eager to learn. He would never forget those years when he listened to O'Halloran's Corkonian brogue and acquired more than a little of that brogue on his own tongue. O'Halloran taught Ned for only a few years, but he taught him well. Many years later O'Halloran would tell everyone he met that he was the first to place a Latin grammar in the hands of Edmund Burke.

At the age of twelve Ned went to Ballitore, a Quaker school in County Kildare. Although Ballitore never attained the fame of the prestigious English preparatory schools, it was superior to such schools in some ways. Students were never caned, nor were the older boys allowed to bully the younger boys. Learning was imparted gently, but it was imparted. Students received a thorough background in the Greek and Latin classics, but the headmaster, Abraham Shackleton, would not allow them to read "those authors who recommend in seducing language the illusions of love and the abominable trade of war."

In a book published in 1748, a few years after Burke was a student at Ballitore, "Two English Gentlemen" indicate how charming the school grounds must have been:

> . . . through the lofty trees, we beheld a variety of pleasant dwellings. Through a road that looked like a fine terrace walk, we turned down to view this lovely vale, where Nature, assisted by Art, gave us the utmost contentment. It is a colony of Quakers, called by the name of Ballitore. The Grise winds its stream very near the houses; and the buildings, orchards and gardens show a neatness peculiar to that people. Their burying-ground, near the road, is surrounded with different trees, whose verdure made us imagine it was a beautiful garden, till better informed. The hedges that inclose their meadows and fields are quick-set, kept of an equal height, and about every ten yards have trees regularly planted, which in a few years will form a beautiful grove of a large extent. Industry seems to reign amongst them, and all their works are executed with a thriving hand.

The happiest years of Ned's life were those he spent at Ballitore. Yet it was shortly after his arrival at Ballitore that he saw the most shocking sight he had ever witnessed. He was walking along a road near the school when he saw an old man weeping bitterly. Ned asked what was the matter, and the old man said that the Surveyor of Roads had torn down his little shack. Ned looked at the ruins and asked a few questions. He found it hard to understand why anyone could do something so cruel.

"But you must have a home!" Ned insisted. "Don't worry. I'll get some other boys, and we'll build you a fine new home."

Ned ran back to the school. Still panting, he knocked on Abraham Shackleton's door. "Come in," said Shackleton. "Ah, Ned!" he added with a smile as the door opened. Ned's outgoing personality and brilliance in his studies had already endeared him to the Shackleton family. But Shackleton's face became concerned as Ned spilled out the story of the poor old man. Still half out of breath, Ned added, "We'll have to build a new house for him. Will you give permission for a few boys to get together and . . . "

Shackleton shook his head sadly. "Twould be of no avail, Ned. The Surveyor of Roads would simply tear down the new shelter."

"Why should he do that? Why should anyone take a poor old man's house away from him, and he with no other place to go? You should see him! It's fair heartbreaking, the way he's shaking and sobbing!"

Tears shimmered in Shackleton's eyes. He would let the old man stay at the school, he said, at least for a few days. But so many people were being evicted all over Ireland that neither Shackleton nor anyone else could do much about the problem.

Later, after the old man had been fed and given a place to sleep, Shackleton spoke with Ned and some of the other boys about the way the Catholics were treated in Ireland. Some of what he said was not entirely new to Ned. Growing up with Catholic relatives and being taught by a Catholic hedge-schoolmaster, Ned had heard the word "eviction" before, but not until he had seen an evicted person did the full horror of the word strike him. Now he understood why Catholics uttered that word with such bitterness.

For some, eviction was a death sentence. No matter what their physical condition — even if they were aged and bedridden, women in labor, newborn babies — they might be thrown out of their pitiful little shelters. Utterly destitute, hungry, and exhausted, some of them died before they could find a bite to eat or shelter from the rain or snow. Those who survived, in despair, would accept any kind of labor at starvation wages.

For weeks after the incident with the evicted man Ned talked about it with Abraham Shackleton's son Richard, who was fifteen and seemed to Ned to be exceptionally well informed. Why did Protestants treat Catholics so cruelly? Protestants weren't just naturally cruel, Ned knew. He himself was a Protestant, as were all his schoolmates. And they wouldn't have been allowed to remain at Ballitore if they had behaved viciously.

One reason why the Catholics were so mistreated, Abraham Shackleton explained to the boys, was that much of the land in Ireland now belonged to absentee landlords. They lived in England and rarely or never visited Ireland. They simply instructed their agents to get as much money as possible from the land. If a Catholic should make even a tiny improvement on his little plot of ground, his rent would be raised beyond his ability to pay. Or if — because of illness, injury, or poor crops — he wasn't able to work as hard as usual, he might fall behind in his rent. Then he was promptly evicted. Protestant landlords who lived in Ireland treated their tenants more kindly. Such landlords knew what their tenants looked like and had witnessed the sufferings of evicted persons. But even those landlords blandly accepted the fact that Catholics must live in dire poverty. Wool, beef, and farm produce raised on Ireland's rich soil were shipped in enormous quantities to England. But the livestock were treated better than the human beings who tended them.

By this time Ned had begun to give serious thought to his future. Like all boys, he wondered what he would do when he grew up. It seemed as natural for a boy to have such thoughts as for a tree to give forth leaves. Everything in nature has an urge to grow until it has developed to its fullest. But Catholics were denied this right to grow. To be a Catholic must be like going around with a weight on one's head — that is, if one happened to be a boy.

For a girl it was different. Ned's sister Juliana, a year older than he, was being brought up as a Catholic, but had the advantage of having a well-to-do Protestant father, and she didn't have to have a career anyway. If she married well, she would be accomplishing as much as could be expected of her. She was a pleasant-mannered, pretty girl to whom Richard Shackleton became romantically attracted. But eventually he married another woman, and she married another man.

During his years at Ballitore Ned became passionately interested in writing. Since Richard Shackleton also loved to write, they would set each other exercises and criticize each other's work. What kind of writing? Usually it was poetry. Neither of them possessed any remarkable poetic gifts, but they had been reading poetry for most of their lives, in Latin and Greek as well as in English, and they enjoyed experimenting with words and ideas. Ned was developing into a thoughtful boy, deeply concerned with what was going on in the world and eager to learn about all sorts of things. Since his limp prevented him from excelling in school athletics, he got most of his exercise by walking or riding horseback around the neat, well-tended grounds of Ballitore. Usually Richard Shackleton was at his side. They would remain lifelong friends, with many interests to share.

In April, 1744, Ned left Ballitore to take the entrance examinations at Trinity College in Dublin, one of the finest institutions of higher learning in the world. Jonathan Swift, the brilliant and scathing Irish satirist of the early eighteenth century, said of Trinity College: "There is a University in Ireland founded by Queen Elizabeth, where youth are instructed with much stricter discipline than in either Oxford or Cambridge."

Like all such institutions, Trinity College was open only to Protestants, and its admission standards were high. But Abraham Shackleton felt confident that Ned, now a gangly youth of fifteen, could pass the entrance examinations with credit.

Ned himself wasn't so sure. There was no way of knowing what questions might be asked on the examination. It would be oral, and the examiners were free to assign passages from a wide range of Latin and Greek classics. Despite the thorough drilling Ned had received in those classics, he couldn't be sure that he would be able to handle the particular passages assigned him.

But it was love for Ballitore rather than apprehension about the examination that made him weep as he looked back at the affectionate faces of the Shackleton family.

He made the journey in a primitive two-wheeled vehicle, drawn by a single horse and driven by a grumpy carman. Ballitore was only thirty miles from Dublin, but the trip took the better part of the day. The carman had to stop here and there along the way to pick up and deliver parcels and letters.

By the time Ned reached the gates of Trinity College it was after midnight. He had to ring for the porter to unlock the gate, and the porter snapped at him for arriving at such an ungodly hour. But he did let Ned in, and Ned went straight to bed in the room that was assigned to him. He was so exhausted from the tedious journey that he fell asleep immediately. After breakfast next morning he met his examiner, Dr. Pellasier, whom he described, in a letter to Richard Shackleton, as "one of the most learned in the university, but an exceedingly good-humored cleanly civil fellow." Dr. Pellasier chatted for a few minutes before starting the examination. Then he asked Ned to translate a few passages from the *Aeneid* and the *Iliad*.

"You are an excellent scholar!" Dr. Pellasier exclaimed."You understand Virgil and Homer very well, and you seem to take pleasure in them. You are more fit for the college than three-fourths of your class."

But the examination wasn't over. Dr. Pellasier said that Ned must also be examined by the Senior Lecturer. Next day Ned appeared before the Senior Lecturer, who gave him a strict examination based on passages from Horace's *Odes, Sermons,* and *Epistles.* The Senior Lecturer was sterner than Dr. Pellasier. He paid no compliments. But Ned knew he had done well when Dr. Pellasier shook his hand and told him that he had been accepted.

In his letter to Richard Shackleton Ned said, "I cannot express, nor have I the knack of doing it, how much I am obliged to your Father for the extraordinary pains and care he has taken with me so as to merit the commendation of my Tutor, and all I can do is to behave myself so as not to bring a scandal upon him or his School."

But he would soon learn that life in Dublin was very different from the pleasant life he had enjoyed at Ballitore.

2. Dublin Years
(1744-1750)

SINCE NED'S FAMILY lived only a short distance from Trinity College, he would be living at home instead of boarding at the college. Bursting with excitement over his success on his entrance examinations, he hurried home to tell the good news. His father and mother greeted him with hugs and kisses, as they always did at their infrequent meetings. The first night at home was jolly, with Ned recounting his experiences at the college in a rapid, emotional voice. His father, in high good humor, made appreciative comments, while his mother looked at him as if he were the eighth wonder of the world.

She was by no means an ignorant woman. Although she was a Catholic, she had enjoyed some educational advantages. But she knew no Latin except for a few prayers, and Greek was a mystery to her. Her fifteen-year-old son seemed to know so much! But he still seemed to her to be too thin and delicate. She didn't feel sure that he had completely regained his health, even after years of living in the country. She would have to be sure that he got plenty of good food. She kept urging him to eat more.

But the first night at home was not typical. Before Ned had been in Dublin more than a day or so he found that the atmosphere at home was always strained. He wondered how his older brother Garrett accepted it so calmly. Garrett was one of the quiet Irish (who are probably at least as common as the hot-tempered Irish but are seldom heard of because they attract so little attention to themselves). He was less brilliant than Ned and would not go so far with his education, although he, too, had attended Ballitore. Garrett had inherited his mother's placid temperament. If he felt any distress over the tensions at home, he didn't show it. He seemed to accept an unhappy situation as something that couldn't be cured and therefore must be endured. (A younger brother, Richard, was attending Ballitore while Ned was in college. Richard was bright, but did not have Ned's serious cast of mind.)

The most disturbing thing about the Burke home was the way Ned's father behaved. He would fly into violent rages and throw wild accusations at everyone. Ned, who had never seen a man behave in such a way during his years at Ballyduff and Ballitore, would watch helplessly while his father raved at a servant's clumsiness or complained about some annoying neighbor.

Ned's father was brilliant. At one time he had been at the top of his profession and had earned a large income. Now, though still well-to-do, he was in decline. His temper had cost him many clients, and the loss of clients had led to more outbursts of temper. He was in failing health and embittered by many disappointments. And he made near-impossible demands on Ned, evidently counting on his most talented son to bring credit to the family by becoming an outstanding success.

Although Ned was now a college man, he was more restricted than when he was only a schoolboy. His father would not allow him to go out after dark and held him strictly accountable for everything that he did during the day. Ned was expected to excel in his studies. Yet he had to do his studying amid the constant distractions at home.

Ned confided to a college friend that "desperate" thoughts sometimes entered his mind. If he could have done so, he would have walked all the way back to Ballitore. Since that was out of the question, he thought of running away from home. Some Irish boys, he had heard, managed to go to America by working their way on board a ship. And stories came back that such boys sometimes did quite well for themselves in America . . .

But he couldn't resort to that way of escape, either. He couldn't bring further distress to his mother, who had no choice but to put up with his father's temper. Her health was poor, and that was not surprising, considering that she had borne fifteen children and seen most of them die in early childhood. A few of the younger children were still living while Ned was in college, but he seldom mentioned them in his letters. Since they were sickly children, no doubt they made the home atmosphere even more difficult for a hard-working college student.

Soon Ned made a practice of studying away from home, spending at least three hours each day in the college library. College courses at Trinity were not nearly so varied as courses in most twentieth-century American colleges. The emphasis was on the Greek and Latin classics, supplemented by a little work in logic, astronomy, and physics. And Ned, who was intrigued by just about everything under the sun, supplemented required reading with much reading of books of his own choice. Assignments were heavy, and there was little time for recreation — except for the socially privileged students, sons of the Anglo-Irish nobility. They did not worry about excelling in their studies. Their position in life was assured, and they attended college merely to acquire a certain polish and to associate with others of their own class. After classes were over for the day, they sallied forth to enjoy the advantages of the brilliant Dublin society.

Ned, who dressed well but not ostentatiously, stared in amazement at the attire of these fine young gentlemen. At Ballitore students had dressed simply. Ned had never seen anything so elegant as the clothes of the high-born students: pleated shirts, ruffled at the wrists, coats with long capes, velvet breeches adorned with silver buckles at the knee, pumps of Spanish leather.

Yet the feeling that he had for such students was not pure envy. He had listened to their conversation and felt dismay at the shallowness of their chatter. They talked about clothes, about the weather, about trivialities in the daily news. He had expected something better than that from college men. Why, when he was a mere boy at Ballitore, he and Dicky Shackleton had talked about far more serious and important subjects.

In spite of the restrictions that his father put on him, Ned could not be prevented from learning a good deal about the city, fascinating to him after years spent in the country. Sometimes he would stroll through the streets near Trinity College, which was located in the center of the aristocratic quarter of the city. Many magnificent mansions had recently been built there — fine brick houses faced with sparkling granite from the nearby Wicklow Hills, with pillared doorways and ornamental fanlights over the doors. The squares and avenues of this section of Dublin were the equal of those in any other city in Europe. And the people who lived in those mansions — the Anglo-Irish nobility — enjoyed a dazzling social life, marked by elaborate balls and banquets. Trinity students were often invited to these homes and allowed to participate in the rich cultural life of Dublin. But during Ned's early college days he was not allowed to enjoy that type of recreation. He heard about concerts and the theater from other students, however, and longed for the time when his father would allow him to go out at night.

Yet there was another side of Dublin life that Ned could not avoid seeing — the life led by the poverty-stricken Irish Catholics. Gap-toothed, pasty-faced, ragged and dirty, they nevertheless displayed spirit and humor. Sometimes Ned heard them chanting ballads deriding the English, and he wondered how they dared to do so. But evidently Catholics were allowed to express themselves in this way so long as they did not engage in riotous behavior. Sticks and stones might break English bones. Ballads hurt nobody.

If Ned ever had reason to feel sorry for himself because of the unhappy conditions at home, he still felt highly privileged compared with the Catholics. Now he could understand why his father, born a Catholic, had renounced his religion and joined the Established Church. Other Catholics had the right to do this, but few ever did. They treasured their faith and chose to live in misery rather than renounce it. But why wasn't it possible to remain a Catholic and at the same time enjoy a rewarding life? Why had the Penal Laws been kept on the books so long?

By this time Ned was old enough to understand why laws were difficult to repeal. Laws made by Protestants could be changed only by Protestants, since no Catholic was allowed to sit in Parliament. Even if some Protestants might wish to change the laws, they could not propose such changes without risking their own careers. Some Protestants might salve their consciences by pointing out that the laws were not strictly enforced. With the passing of the years many infringements of the laws were overlooked. But what this meant was that, whenever it was convenient, the laws could be enforced with frightful consequences to the victims.

(It should be noted that the word "Protestant" includes Presbyterians as well as members of the Established Church. The majority of Irish Protestants were Presbyterians. Members of the Established Church exercised a social and political ascendancy over the Presbyterians similar to that which Protestants in general exercised over the Catholics. Presbyterians were not, like the Catholics, deprived of the right to vote, but they had little political influence and were almost unrepresented in Irish Parliament. The Irish Parliament, in fact, represented only a minority of a minority of the Irish people.)

Although Ned was only fifteen, he was unusually serious-minded. In letters to Richard Shackleton he expressed concern over things that had attracted his attention in Dublin. Only a few months after he entered college he told Richard that he would like to form a club for serious discussion. First he had to find a few other students who shared his interests.

In May, 1746, he was so elated over winning a scholarship that he wrote to Richard immediately, telling him about the difficult two-day examination that he had taken in order to qualify for the honor. One of the examiners was so impressed with his performance, he said, that the examiner wanted to know what school he had attended. Ned was proud to say that he had attended Ballitore. Scholarship-winners, besides getting free room and board, were allowed fifty shillings' worth of wine a year and were given three to four pounds a year to pay for such necessities as fuel, candles, and salt. Besides, there was great prestige in being a Trinity Scholar. Scholars wore a special type of academic gown, and Ned was going to buy such a gown as soon as he finished writing the letter.

But his father was not pleased with the news. He didn't want Ned to live away from home. The cash value of the scholarship wasn't important. Ned's father could afford to pay his son's college expenses, even though he kept grumbling about them. Ned had to use all his powers of persuasion to convince his father of the advantages of accepting the scholarship. The fact that the scholarship was an honor was a strong argument, also the fact that it might help him in his later career. His father gave in, but with the stipulation that Ned must continue to make frequent visits home.

Only a few weeks later Ned had sadder news to report to Richard Shackleton. His mother became so ill that for three days her death was expected momentarily. Ned watched desperately as the grave-faced doctor came and went. The priest came to administer the last rites, and servants and relatives knelt to intone the sorrowful mysteries of the rosary. The mournful cadence of voices rising and falling in Our Fathers and Hail Marys sent a horrible shudder through Ned. In his letter to Richard, Ned apologized for not having written recently, saying that he had never in his life known so heavy a grief. During those critical days he felt too weak to hold a pen. Fortunately, his mother recovered and went to County Cork to recuperate. She would live on for many years.

After his mother recovered, Ned began to revel in his new freedom. Now he could enjoy some of the more stimulating side of college life. In April, 1747, he carried out his plan for forming a club. With six other students he founded a Debating Club, which would meet regularly to discuss such matters as morality, history, literary criticism, politics, and "all the useful branches of philosophy." They criticized each other's arguments and manner of delivery and thus sharpened their skill in using the spoken word. (Notebooks containing the minutes of these meetings are now among the treasures preserved in the manuscript room of Trinity College Library. In time this little club developed into the Trinity College Historical Society, whose members achieved worldwide fame for their skill in debating.)

There are references in the club minutes to criticisms made of Ned's contributions. He was praised for the "matter" (that is, the content) of his arguments but criticized for speaking too rapidly and emotionally. He criticized others in turn, and his comments could be cutting. At one meeting one member charged him with being "damned absolute" in his opinions. No member took the club so seriously as Ned. He was never absent or late, and he had no patience with those who were lax about attendance. Richard Shackleton was later admitted to the club, and his absences were the only ones that Ned excused — not because Richard was his dear friend, but because he lived in Ballitore and could attend meetings only during visits to Dublin.

Now Ned was able to attend the theater, and he developed such a passion for it that he thought of becoming a dramatist. If it delighted him to listen to the words of other dramatists, spoken by the world's finest actors, how much greater that delight would be if he could sit in the audience and hear his own words spoken and applauded! But it was not simply the words of the plays that thrilled him. It was the whole glamorous atmosphere of the playhouse, lighted by hundreds of candles and filled with spectators from all walks of life. Since many theater seats cost very little, even streetsweepers could afford to attend, and the common people loved the theater. Those who couldn't afford even the cheapest tickets could stand outside and watch the aristocrats arriving in elegant coaches or sedan chairs.

Ned never did become a dramatist, but his passion for the theater would remain with him for the rest of his days. Some of his closest friends in later years would be actors and playwrights.

A fellow student of Ned's at Trinity College would one day write plays that are being performed to this day. But nobody would have predicted a brilliant future for that student during his college days.

Oliver Goldsmith attended Trinity College at the same time as Ned, but they moved in different orbits. While Ned stood at or near the top scholastically, Goldsmith barely scraped through. Aside from the difference in their scholastic standing, there were other reasons they would not have had much to do with each other. Ned may well have been a bit of a snob. It would have been difficult not to be a snob in a college setting in which social differences were sharply defined. As the son of a prosperous professional man, he just wouldn't have been likely to associate with a student as poor as Goldsmith.

As was customary in all colleges at the time, even in America, students were treated differently according to their social rank. At Trinity there were five social ranks: noblemen, untitled younger sons of noblemen, fellow-commoners, pensioners, and sizars. Goldsmith was a sizar.

Sizars paid a nominal sum for a miserable room in a garret and got free board and tuition. They were expected to sweep the college courtyard, scrub floors, carry dishes from the kitchen to the dinner table. They ate only after the other students had finished and thus had no opportunity to participate in the table conversations that are an important part of college life. To make their rank visible at a glance, sizars were required to wear long sleeveless gowns of coarse black cloth and red caps, the red cap being the sign of a servant.

This grotesque garb did nothing to improve Goldsmith's appearance, which would under no circumstances have seemed prepossessing. His brow was abnormally high, his sallow skin was pock-marked, and he was slight in build. His humorous outlook on life led him to smile more than, as a sizar, he had a right to do. Such qualities can irritate some professors. And Goldsmith had the misfortune to have as his College Tutor the Reverend Theaker Wilder, as vicious a professorial bully as ever presided over a classroom. Although Goldsmith had a singularly sweet disposition, he characterized Wilder as "the most depraved, profligate, and licentious being in human shape."

Even a student as brilliant as Ned had trouble with Wilder. In letters to Richard Shackleton, Ned sometimes mentioned Wilder's sadistic practice of trying to make students look like idiots on oral examinations. Wilder sometimes prevented Ned from making a good showing on such examinations by sharply asking questions on trivial points and giving Ned no fair opportunity to show how well prepared he was.

Goldsmith couldn't have won Wilder's favor, no matter how hard he tried. Goldsmith didn't try too hard. He had a genius for getting into precisely the kind of trouble that would infuriate Wilder. While Ned received only one academic reprimand at Trinity (for missing a lecture at the time when he was busy organizing the Debating Club), Goldsmith was constantly in hot water for having violated some college rule. His "perpetual lounging about the college gate" was noted in the records as one of his more disgusting offenses — understandably, since a student who looked like Goldsmith could easily give the college a bad name. Yet, if Goldsmith failed to win distinction at the college, he did win a following among the townspeople. He sometimes composed ballads, taking more pleasure in hearing his words sung in the streets and alleys of Dublin than in the five shillings he earned for each ballad.

Goldsmith tried to compete for the kind of scholarship that Ned had won, but was unsuccessful. Still, he managed to rank seventeenth out of nineteen candidates for such a scholarship, and for this achievement was awarded a tiny prize worth thirty shillings a year. He decided to give a party in his room to celebrate. Not only that, but he invited a few women of unsavory reputation to add spice to the party. Another student informed Wilder about the party, and Wilder burst into the room and gave Goldsmith a savage beating.

Poor Goldsmith had taken all he could from his vicious tutor. Next day he sold his books and left the college. He walked from Dublin to Cork, hoping that he might make his way to America by getting work aboard some ship. But he was soon penniless and starving. An older brother came to his rescue, fed and clothed him, and persuaded him to return to college. The brother, a graduate of Trinity, managed to work out some sort of reconciliation between Goldsmith and Wilder, and Goldsmith managed to submit to Wilder's brutality long enough to acquire a degree.

(Today, at either side of the path leading to the main gate of Trinity College, statues of Goldsmith and Burke gaze out at one of Dublin's busiest thoroughfares.)

Ned took his A.B. degree on February 28, 1748, at the age of nineteen. Then, as a Trinity Scholar, he was allowed to live on at the college for some months. He thought of becoming a don. But eventually he decided, "He that lives in a college, after his mind is sufficiently stocked with learning, is like a man who, having built and rigged and victualled a ship, should lock her up in a dry dock." Even before his studies at Trinity College ended, he had applied for admission to the Middle Temple in London to study law. But he did not leave for London until 1750. Meanwhile he wrote articles for a periodical called *The Reformer,* expressing his opinions of literature, the theater, and social problems. An indication of his great concern for the plight of the Irish Catholics is given in one of these articles:

> . . . As for their Food, it is notorious that they seldom taste Bread or Meat; their Diet in Summer is Potatoes and sour Milk; in Winter . . . they are still worse, living on the same Root only palatable by a little Salt. . . . Their Cloathes so ragged that they rather publish than conceal the Wretchedness it was meant to hide; nay, it is no uncommon sight to see half a dozen Children run quite naked out of a Cabin scarcely distinguishable from a Dunghill. . . . You enter, or rather creep in, at a Door of Hurdles plastered with Dirt, of which the Inhabitant is generally the Fabricator, within-side you see (if the Smoke will permit you) the Men, Women, Children, Dogs, and Swine lying promiscuously, for their Opulence is such that they cannot have a separate House for their Cattle, as it would take too much from the Garden, whose produce is their only Support. Their Furniture is much fitter to be lamented than described, such as a Pot, a Stool, a few wooden Vessels, and a broken bottle. In this manner all the Peasantry, to a Man, live, and I Appeal to any one, who knows the Country, for the Justness of the Picture.

After describing the luxury in which the wealthy lived, he said:

> But the Riches of a Nation are not to be estimated by the splendid Appearance or luxurious Lives of the Gentry; it is the uniform Plenty diffused through a People of which the meanest as well as greatest partake that makes them happy, and the Nation powerful. It is the care of every wise Government to secure the Lives and Property of those who live under it; why should it be less worthy of consideration to make those

Lives comfortable and their Properties worth preserving? That some should live in a more sumptuous Manner than others is very allowable, but sure it is hard that those who cultivate the Soil should have so small a part in its Fruits, and that among Creatures of the same Kind there should be such a disproportion in their manner of living. It is a kind of Blasphemy on Providence.

These words, written by a youth not yet turned twenty-one, indicate a deep concern for the oppressed. But they do not glow with fiery indignation. They are not the words of one so disturbed by existing social conditions that he would advocate drastic changes. It could be that the original draft of the essay was more impassioned, since Ned was highly emotional. Speaking extemporaneously, he was often carried away by the intensity of his feelings. Possibly the original draft was watered down by a cautious editor — and possibly not. Ned had a deep respect for traditions that had been handed down over the generations. The existing class system as such did not trouble him. Anyway, what could he do about it beyond calling attention to some of its defects?

More because of his father's desires than because of his own, he would soon leave for London to prepare himself for a career as a lawyer. Given a free choice, he would have preferred to be a writer. But a writing career was risky, whereas a good lawyer could always make a good living. And maybe he would not have to spend the rest of his life handling petty lawsuits. Maybe, in the dazzling world of London, he would find a way to fulfill his destiny as a writer.

3. Irish Greenhorn in England
(1750)

EDMUND BURKE WAS neither penniless nor friendless when he arrived in London. His father had provided him with an allowance large enough to meet all sensible needs. His father had also arranged for him to stay at the home of a lawyer kinsman, John Burke. There would be no starving in a garret for the brilliant young son of a prosperous Dublin lawyer, no days of wandering forlornly through a city of strangers. Life in London would not be painful for Edmund Burke as it is for many young people arriving in a big city to seek their fortunes. But life would not be easy, either. Life would never be easy for Edmund Burke.

Still, it was pleasant enough for a time, chiefly because his cousin, Will Burke, was friendly. Will, a graduate of Oxford University, had good looks, charm, the assurance of one who knows his way around. Other qualities in his personality were less apparent on short acquaintance. He was shallow, opportunistic, full of dreams of getting rich without having to exert himself unduly. As Edmund came to know Will better, those traits must have become evident, but by that time Edmund was so fond of Will that he could overlook a few character blemishes. Will was to have a strong influence on Edmund — for bad as well as good — for the rest of their lives.

Even without Will's help, Edmund would have made friends in London eventually. He had a remarkable gift for making friends and would form many interesting associations over the years, while still remaining loyal to the friends of his youth. Yet he formed no lasting friendships among his fellow students at the Middle Temple.

Possibly the other law students found him gauche and comical. He was never one to keep his mouth shut very long. He was full of opinions, and he couldn't resist expressing those opinions even to those who might find them boring or distasteful. No doubt he talked too much when, as a newcomer, he would have been more prudent to hold his tongue. Students at the Middle Temple were required to take their dinners there, since one of the most meaningful features of their law course was table conversation. Possibly, at his first few dinners, Burke was naively enthusiastic about things that he had seen in London. He had walked across the new Westminster Bridge, gaping at the two solid towers of Westminster Abbey, the huge buildings of Mayfair and Piccadilly, the gleaming white Royal Stables at Charing Cross. He had leaned on the rail to look at the great barges, the clippers, the host of small craft on the Thames. He had sat in the visitors' gallery of the House of Commons, amazed at the "explosions of eloquence" from the speakers. And he wanted to tell everyone what he had seen and done.

The other Middle Temple students looked at each other with superior amusement. Most of them came from extremely wealthy families. They dressed ostentatiously and spent money freely. In various ways they showed that they regarded Burke as "poor," for all that he was the son of a prosperous Irish lawyer. His enthusiasm about tourist attractions seemed rather vulgar. He had never learned to play card games. He didn't know how to dance. He spoke with an Irish brogue that jarred the sensibilities of highborn Englishmen.

Since a pronounced regional accent could be a great handicap to young men eager to rise in the world, they often took elocution lessons. Burke probably took such lessons with an actor named Charles Macklin, for he recommended Macklin to a Scotsman named Alexander Wedderburn, who would in time become a lord chancellor of England. But if Burke did indeed take such a course, it doesn't seem to have helped much in eliminating his brogue. The Irish brogue differs, of course, from one county to another. Since Burke spent his early years in Dublin, in County Cork, and in County Kildare, his accent may have been a mixture. At any rate, it would have been agreed by all who knew him that he had a brogue nothing but death could extinguish.

Even worse than his silly enthusiasm for London was his choice of subjects to discuss at the dinner table. Knowing that some of his fellow students were the sons of wealthy Southern planters from the American colonies, knowing that the families of some of the English students had grown wealthy from the slave trade, he had the poor taste to denounce slavery. Well, he was young, in time he might acquire better control of his emotions and learn to be more discreet about expressing his opinions. Meanwhile he could hardly expect the other students to admit him to their more intimate circles or to listen patiently while he tried to dominate the conversation.

Burke did listen, of course. Fond as he was of the sound of his own voice, he did like to hear the opinions of others. Just as he had looked for a few students at Trinity College who had a serious cast of mind, he now looked for students who might be able to teach him things about the law that he could not discover for himself by poring over dusty tomes in the well-stocked library. But his dinner table companions seemed to be chiefly interested in learning how to use legal tricks, how to set up a lucrative practice. They never spoke about the law as a means of improving the lot of mankind. Burke's fellow students didn't seem to care about that sort of thing. They wanted a profession that would bring them a good income and prestige. Like his fellow students, Burke wanted success. He wanted to earn enough to live in comfort. But he wanted more. His youthful idealism, nurtured in a Quaker preparatory school, had filled him with an urge to use his God-given talents in a way that would make the world a better place. He longed for something that he couldn't seem to get from any of his fellow students.

For the kind of conversation that really stimulated him, he turned to the coffeehouses, where men gathered to share ideas and express opinions. Coffeehouses sold other beverages besides coffee, both alcoholic and nonalcoholic. But their attraction was not the refreshments — it was the fact that they functioned much like clubs, at a cost so modest that even a young law student on a skimpy allowance could easily afford them. This form of socializing was common in eighteenth-century London, not only for men with no domestic ties but for men of all conditions. It was a gregarious age, a time when men richly enjoyed the stimulus of conversation with anyone they might happen to meet at a coffeehouse.

At a cost of no more than twopence, a man might linger over a mug of tea or coffee, reading newspapers and pamphlets or discussing the issues of the day with those who shared his table. The atmosphere was heartily masculine, with the odor of coffee beans being roasted, whorls of blue-gray smoke rising from long white clay pipes, the rumble of men's voices. Some coffeehouses catered chiefly to one type of client — writers or students, landed gentry or workingmen.

In other coffeehouses lords and shoemakers, tailors and merchants might share the same table and openly discuss politics. Foreigners visiting England were amazed that such talk, which even included ridicule of the royal family, should be allowed to go on without the authorities interfering.

In the coffeehouses Burke was in his element. He was sufficiently well informed to be interesting to the other men who gathered there, but he was also learning things about the English way of life. Yes, and the American way of life too, for sometimes he met Americans at the coffeehouses or men who had visited America.

Burke longed to go to America. Opportunities for advancement were so great there. Land was so plentiful that it cost little or nothing. It was not, as in England, in the hands of a few enormously wealthy families. And since there was no noble class in America, talented men of relatively humble birth often rose to high positions. All of this Burke found appealing. In America he could use his talents to the fullest. One day he might go there. But first he must complete his law studies.

Besides visiting coffeehouses, Burke liked to drop in at the Robin Hood Tavern, a place frequented by law students, shopkeepers, artisans, and professional men. There, for a fee of sixpence, he could enjoy a glass of lemonade or a jug of porter and have the privilege of debating the topic of the evening. This experience in matching wits with untrained but natively keen minds undoubtedly helped him to improve his skills as a debater.

Will Burke sometimes took Edmund for excursions into the countryside. Edmund was enormously impressed with the majestic estates, the flourishing farms, the gracious inns. The natural beauties of England were actually no greater than those of his native Ireland, but the serenity of the English countryside was not marred by the sight of peasants living in squalor or hobbling along the road after an eviction.

There were poor people in England. Indeed, most of the people in England were poor. But the English poor were less visible than the Irish poor. Many, finding it impossible to survive in the country, flocked to the cities, where they lived in slums of the vilest type. But the English had ways of disposing of their poor when they became too numerous. To save the cost of keeping them in poorhouses or prisons, the authorities shipped them to America. The ships on which those unfortunates traveled took ten to twelve weeks to cross the Atlantic, and conditions on those ships were so horrible that about half of the passengers perished on the way. But once a former convict or pauper landed in America, he had more cause for hope than he would ever have enjoyed in England. He would have to work as a bondservant for several years to repay the cost of his transportation. But once that debt was worked off, he could clear a plot in the forest and build a home. Nearly everything that he needed could be obtained from the forest — lumber to build a house and make furniture; food; clothing made from the skins of animals. He could earn enough income for other needs by selling farm produce and animal pelts. With a large family to help him and reasonable luck in avoiding illness or injury, he could in time become a highly respected person. As a property-owner, he could even enjoy the right to vote, a right enjoyed by only a tiny proportion of Englishmen.

Burke listened with concern as Will Burke told him about the English method of dealing with the problem of poverty. But it was impossible for Burke to regard a statistic as an abstract figure. When he heard that half the passengers on the prison ships died during passage, he actually visualized human beings in the throes of dying. He saw dead bodies being tossed into the ocean. On his return to London he talked about transportation ships with men in the coffeehouses. From them he learned that the estimate of half the passengers dying was probably low. The misery of those passengers was appalling. They were devoured by lice, driven mad by heat and thirst. The moans and ravings of the dying and demented made sleep impossible for the rest. Shipwrecks were frequent. A sentence of transportation was considered so terrifying that convicts, hearing themselves condemned to such a sentence, often let out cries of agony or collapsed. Burke listened to such stories with tears in his eyes. Concealing his emotions had never been part of his nature. He felt both sorrow and joy more intensely than most men.

Oh, he did know joy in England — especially when he went to the theater. Since some seats were available at low prices, he could afford to attend performances from time to time. On evenings when he did not have a ticket, it was exciting to stroll around Covent Garden just for the pleasure of observing the strange assortment of characters who gathered there at night. Peddlers hawking patent medicines. Women selling flowers, fruits, and vegetables. Beggars — blind, crippled, disfigured — swarming from the nearby dismal alleys. Pickpockets, who plied their trade wherever a crowd gathered, unconcerned that, if caught, they might be hanged or sentenced to transportation. The risk was worth it. A gold watch or a jewel-encrusted snuff-box could bring in enough money for some few years of comfort.

What fascinated Burke most about Covent Garden were the young dandies arriving in ornate coaches or sedan chairs. Oh, the la-de-da airs they put on! The smugness of their silly faces! The disdainful way they flicked back the lace ruffles on their wrists. They must have spent hours before a mirror while their valets fluttered about, arranging the curls of a powdered wig, adjusting a tricornered hat to precisely the right tilt, hanging a dress sword with a studiously casual air. Burke couldn't take his eyes off the dandies. Empty-noodled and vain though they were, they had everything handed to them on a silver platter. All doors were opened to them. They could attend the theater whenever they felt so inclined or squander a fortune in a single evening at a gambling table.

Sometimes, looking at the dandies, Burke felt actually ill. Why were they free to lead idle, useless lives while he must plug away at his studies before he could begin to earn a living? Something more than envy was gnawing at him. He felt again the helplessness that he had felt years ago when his mother was on the verge of death. His grief at that time was understandable. But now he had no obvious reason for feeling such weakness.

He was suffering from a malady known in those days as "melancholia," a condition so common among the English at that time that it was called "the English disease." Today this condition in its extreme form might be diagnosed as manic-depressive psychosis; in a less extreme form it would be considered neurotic depression. Burke's symptoms were probably not unlike those of ambitious young people of today who arrive in a big city bursting with a desire to succeed, only to find themselves unwanted. Today, people suffering from depression might consult a psychiatrist or a psychologist. Psychotherapy as such was unknown in the eighteenth century, but a few wise doctors did know something about the interplay between mind and body, and they practiced something resembling psychotherapy. Burke was fortunate enough to find such a doctor in Bath, a health resort about a hundred miles west of London.

4. Romance and First Literary Success
(1750-1758)

DR. CHRISTOPHER NUGENT was an Irish Catholic widower with a son and daughter a few years younger than Burke. He had spent a good part of his youth in Europe, studied medicine in Belgium and France, and acquired a cosmopolitan background unusual for doctors of his time and exceptional for an Irish Catholic. This background undoubtedly stood him in good stead in a place like Bath, where the wealthiest people in England came to bathe in the medicinal springs and drink the curative waters. Nugent seems to have been one of those doctors who care more about easing human misery than about getting rich. He was well read, compassionate, generous. And he may have charged young Burke little or nothing. Burke stayed at the Nugent home while undergoing treatment.

The thing that most impressed him about that home was its tranquil atmosphere. After years of living in a Dublin home where one hot-tempered man could distress the entire household, Burke found it bliss to live with people of gentle manners. Dr. Nugent's son Jack and daughter Jane were as kind as Nugent himself and treated Burke as if he were a dear relative rather than a patient.

Burke had never known a girl like Jane. Until this time he had associated chiefly with youths of his own age and had been too busy with his studies to ''waste time'' with women. Now he realized what he had been missing. Jane was an auburn-haired beauty of sixteen, the most attractive girl he had ever seen. Everything about her delighted him: her soft voice, the glow of intelligence on her winsome face, her graceful way of walking. In short, he was in love, and the object of his love was a creature free of blemish. He tried putting into words what it was about her that made him catch his breath and flush whenever she entered a room: "She is handsome, but it is a beauty not arising from features, from complexion and shape. She has all these in a high degree, but whoever looks at her never perceives them, nor makes them the topic of his praises. 'Tis all the sweetness of temper, benevolence, innocence and sensibility which a face can express, that forms her beauty."

He wanted to marry her. Ambitious as he had been when he arrived in London some six months earlier, he was now doubly ambitious to become rich and famous so that he could give Jane everything her heart might desire. But it was this very ambition that had led to his depression when he discovered how difficult it would be to achieve his goals. Nugent had long talks with him and helped him to take a more philosophical attitude toward life. But the problems that had brought Burke to Bath in the first place were now accentuated by his feelings about Jane. He couldn't ask her to marry him. He had no money but the allowance from his father.

Jane was rather young for marriage, of course. But would she be willing to wait until Edmund could afford marriage? In Bath she could easily meet men far wealthier, far more distinguished than a lanky young law student. The social life of Bath was elaborate. Patrons of the baths attended concert breakfasts, balls, plays, card parties, banquets. At certain hours it was their custom to stroll in the meadows or along the banks of the Avon River. Romance flourished. Indeed, mothers often brought their daughters to Bath to make a good match. Would Jane, for all that she seemed to possess uncommon common sense, be carried away by the blandishments of some young man more dazzlingly handsome than Burke, some young man from a wealthy family or a man with a more established position? The thought was torture. Burke must find a way to convince her that he was worthy of her.

He could not afford to remain in Bath very long after his first meeting with the Nugents. He had to return to London to plug away at his law studies. But he returned to Bath from time to time and strengthened his friendship with the Nugents. And before long Jane revealed that she was attracted to him. Yes, she would wait until he was ready to marry. Her assurance filled Burke with new vigor. Nothing that he could ever do would repay the great debt that he owed to the Nugents, but in 1752 he tried to express his gratitude in a poem to Dr. Nugent:

> Perhaps I drive too fast in this Career,
> And you, good Sir, may whisper in my Ear
> That those who willingly run down a Hill,
> Are forced to run yet more against their Will,
> So men oft hearted with conceits they love
> Prove more, by half, than does them good to prove. . .
> Yet under Planets so perverse are born,
> They wish to be the very things they scorn.
> That Sage, who calls a fop mankind's disgrace,
> Envies that Fop his figure and his face;
> And I, who think it is the time's reproach,
> To see a Scoundrel Gamester in his Coach,
> Think modestly 'twould have a better air,
> To see my humble self exalted there. . .
> 'Tis now two Autumns, since he chanc'd to find,
> A youth of Body broke, infirm of mind,
> He gave him all that man can ask or give,
> Restor'd his life and taught him how to Live.

If this is a representative sample of Burke's poetic talent, the world lost little when he stopped writing poetry. Yet the lines are not without merit. They do say much in few words, and Burke could benefit from practice in trying to express himself with the restrictions imposed by rhyme and rhythm.

Back in London he continued to pore over law books. But he was becoming increasingly dismayed at the way lawyers misused their knowledge. At the Middle Temple emphasis was placed on legal forms and procedures. The students seemed to care nothing for the principles on which law is based. Justice meant less to them than learning ways to pervert justice.

The desire to write still gnawed at Burke. If only he could turn out a book that would bring him fame and fortune! Then he could marry Jane and spend the rest of his life working at a profession that he truly enjoyed. But London was teeming with hopeful young writers, most of whom could hardly keep body and soul together. Instead of producing immortal works of literature, they did hack writing, selling their skill with words to anyone who would pay them a pittance.

Burke now became a hack writer. His knowledge of the law was a great asset in composing pamphlets for Members of Parliament who lacked the talent, the time, or the inclination to do their own writing. Such writing paid poorly, and it was of no use in establishing a literary reputation. The pamphlets were published under the names of those who paid for them. Nobody knew, nobody cared, who had done the actual writing. If Burke continued to work as a hack writer, he'd get nowhere. To establish a literary reputation, he would have to publish something under his own name.

In 1756, when he was twenty-seven, he published the first pamphlet for which he could take full credit: *A Vindication of Natural Society, or a View of the Miseries and Evils Arising in Mankind from Every Species of Civil Society.* It was a satirical discussion of the romantic nature-worship associated with the French philosopher Jean-Jacques Rousseau, and it set out to prove precisely the opposite of what the title implied. Burke was strongly opposed to the notion that the savage is a finer specimen of humanity than civilized man. It was unfortunate that civilized men had many imperfections, but that did not mean that one should therefore discard the trappings of civilization and revert to the "natural" state.

Burke had seen abundant evidence of the evils of civilization in both Ireland and England. One passage from this pamphlet indicates his distress over the sufferings of those who are forced to do unrewarding work in a civilized society:

> I suppose that there are in Great Britain upwards of a hundred thousand people employed in lead, tin, iron, copper, and coal mines; these unhappy wretches scarce ever see the light of the sun; they are buried in the bowels of the earth; there they work at a severe and dismal task, without the least prospect of being delivered from it; they subsist upon the coarsest and worst sort of fare; they have their health miserably impaired, and their lives cut short, by being perpetually confined in the close vapour of these malignant minerals. A hundred thousand more at least are tortured without remission by the suffocating smoke, intense fires, and constant drudgery necessary in refining and managing the products of those mines. If any man informed us that two hundred thousand innocent persons were condemned to so intolerable slavery, how should we pity the unhappy sufferers, and how great would be our indignation against those who inflicted so cruel and ignominious a punishment!

But how should such evils be corrected? Certainly not by discarding all the benefits of civilization. Burke did wish it were possible to change some existing conditions. He could not be complacent about the sufferings of others simply because he himself had been spared such sufferings. But he saw no quick and easy way of bringing about changes for the better. Civilization had not brought happiness to man, but it had brought benefits too valuable to be recklessly discarded.

This pamphlet, which sold for one shilling sixpence, did not enrich its author. Still, it was far more successful than most pamphlets, and people wanted to know more about its author. Burke had now begun to establish himself as something of a personage, and he was listened to with greater respect in coffeehouses. On the strength of such limited success, he decided to give up his law studies and become a writer — and marry Jane. They were married on March 12, 1757. He was twenty-eight. She was twenty-three.

There are no records indicating clearly whether Jane was, like her father, a Roman Catholic. Nugent's marriage, like that of Burke's parents, could have been a union between a Catholic and a Protestant. If so, Jane would have been raised in her mother's religion. No record has been found of the place where Burke and Jane were married, and we do not know what sort of ceremony was performed.

But what about the father back in Dublin, impatiently awaiting the return of the son on whose education he had invested several thousand pounds? How would he react when he heard that his son had decided not to become a lawyer? As might be expected, the elder Burke flew into a rage. Some malicious person had taken the trouble to inform him that his son was infatuated with a Catholic woman and had become converted to Catholicism! Frantic with frustration at being unable to do much about this state of affairs, the father did the one thing he could do. He cut off Edmund's allowance. He wanted no further dealings with such an ungrateful son.

Burke was distressed. He had always been loyal to all of his relatives. Indeed he carried loyalty to such lengths that he refused to see any faults in them. He would never have been guilty of ingratitude. As for the story that he had become a Catholic, there wasn't a word of truth in it. Now he had to convince his father that the expensive education had not been wasted. A second pamphlet, published on April 12, 1757, persuaded the Dublin attorney that his son was actually doing something more admirable than setting up a law practice. The elder Burke was so delighted with the second pamphlet, so proud at being able to boast about his son's achievements, that the breach was healed. In a burst of generosity, he offered the newlyweds an allowance of two hundred pounds a year.

The second pamphlet was entitled *A Philosophical Enquiry into the Origin of Our Ideas of the Sublime and the Beautiful.* Today a book with such a title would have slim chance of winning friends and influencing people, but it was the sort of thing that eighteenth-century readers adored. Those who prided themselves on their intellectual accomplishments discussed it in drawing rooms and invited the young author to their gatherings. The pamphlet remained in print for many years and was translated into several languages. Later it became a source of inspiration to the Romantic poets of the nineteenth century. A surprising thing about it was that Burke wrote the original draft when he was only nineteen. The 1757 version was an updating of ideas that he had been mulling over for many years.

At about this time Burke also had a hand in a book that was published anonymously. It was a two-volume work entitled *An Account of the European Settlements in America,* a history of English, Spanish, French, and Portuguese colonies in the New World. Will Burke, Edmund said, did most of the writing. But Burke's interest in this subject at this stage of his life is significant. He was learning a great deal about the American colonies. In time he would become one of England's foremost authorities on the subject.

An Account of the European Settlements in America was not particularly well written. It gave signs of having been hastily slapped together, perhaps to cash in on the timely interest in the Seven Years' War. It was evidently a financial success, for a second edition appeared seven months after its original publication, and it was reprinted several times during the next twenty years. Although it was poorly researched, it did display remarkable breadth of vision. The author spoke approvingly of the humanitarian efforts of the Catholic clergy and denounced the mistreatment of Indians and black slaves. In discussing British policy toward the colonies, the author pleaded for recognition of the unity of sentiments and interests between the people of Great Britain and those of her colonies. Burke may have had a greater hand in this book than he cared to admit — possibly because he was aware of its defects, possibly because he wanted Will Burke to get the credit for its merits.

It so happens that Burke was thinking seriously of settling in America. He couldn't go there immediately, since England was then at war with France. And the outcome of that war would determine whether France or England would gain dominance in North America. But Burke's desire to go to America was more than a passing whim. Four years later he was still talking about his plans to go there. His father's objections may have been the main reason he never carried out those plans.

After Jane and Edmund were married, they lived with Dr. Nugent, who obligingly moved to London to set up a new practice. Edmund's younger brother Richard came over from Ireland about that time and stayed with them. So did Will Burke. Jane's brother Jack, who would later marry Edmund's cousin Lucy Nagle, was another member of the household. With several adult males contributing to the expenses, they lived in considerable comfort. Friends who visited Burke's home at this period of his life were impressed with its atmosphere of cozy informality.

In 1758 Jane bore two sons: Richard, born on February 9, and Christopher, born on December 14. During the same year Burke took on an assignment that would occupy him for many years. The bookseller Robert Dodsley, who had published Burke's pamphlets, asked him to edit the *Annual Register*, a yearly review of contemporary politics and literature. The pay was only a hundred pounds a year, and the articles were unsigned. But the job gave Burke an opportunity to keep abreast of the important issues of the day. He spent much time in the gallery of the House of Commons, acquiring material for articles, and also attended gatherings where he met influential people.

Things were going well for Burke as he neared his thirtieth birthday. He was happily married and the father of two fine little boys. He had acquired a reputation as a writer and made some friends in London. But the most interesting friendships were still to come.

Only a few days after his second son was born he was invited to have Christmas dinner at the home of the famous actor David Garrick. There he met the redoubtable Samuel Johnson.

5. Literary and Political Friendships
(1758-1765)

EVERY WRITER IN London had heard of Samuel Johnson, a man of such formidable learning and such peculiar mannerisms that young men usually stammered imbecilities upon meeting him. He had opinions about everything, and woe betide the person who tried to contradict him.

Yet at this Christmas dinner in 1758 Edmund Burke blandly contradicted Johnson on several points. The other guests sat dumbfounded, waiting for the famous Johnson bellow. Johnson did not bellow. At last he had met a man who could outtalk him! Instead of being offended, he acted as if he had been waiting all his life for such a man.

One reason for this strange situation was the setting. It was Christmas Day, a day when good Christian men rejoice. And both Johnson and Burke, though in different ways, were religious. Johnson — surprisingly superstitious for one so erudite — may well have believed that he would have violated the sanctity of Christmas had he behaved in his ordinary weekday manner on such a day. There was another reason why Johnson felt inclined to be gracious on this occasion. Garrick, an extraordinarily successful actor, set a superlative table. Johnson, who had sometimes walked the streets all night, unable to pay for a night's lodging, always ate heartily — no, ravenously I when a good meal was set before him. Besides, the subject under discussion was India. Johnson knew little about India and made several inaccurate statements. Burke knew much about India and was eager to impart that knowledge.

People of intellectual pretensions never got far with Johnson. He could pulverize them with one stinging rebuke. But he was quick to discern true ability. Like most creative people, he judged others by personal qualities, not wealth and pedigree. Burke's Irish brogue, his emotional flow of language, his awkward gestures — traits that might have made him a laughingstock in some London drawing rooms — made Johnson glow with appreciation.

Johnson, now aged forty-nine, was no longer desperately poor. But he had not outgrown the slovenly habits developed in earlier days. His rusty brown suit was always stained with food slobbered from an overloaded fork. His rumpled neckcloth always needed laundering. His black worsted stockings hung in wrinkles about his legs. He stuffed his pockets with such oddities as a collection of dried orange peels. His little old shriveled, unpowdered wig was usually singed down to the network because he held his head too close to the candle when reading. He was six feet tall, broad-shouldered, thick-necked. His pale blue eyes at times had an expression so wild and piercing as to strike terror in those who did not know him well. He was blind in one eye, deaf in one ear, disfigured with scrofula. He spoke in a deep bass voice and had dismaying nervous mannerisms: He blinked and puffed, clucked his tongue, rolled his head, drummed with his fingers. His temper was so short that he sometimes came to blows with those who offended him.

Yet he could be extremely courteous. And if he spoke in a terrifying voice and expressed opinions dogmatically, what he had to say was expressed in short, emphatic, well-balanced sentences. Indeed he spoke better than he wrote. He was fundamentally generous. Though he was now far from well-to-do, he made his home a haven for several unfortunate creatures who had no other place to go but the workhouse.

In 1755 he published a *Dictionary of the English Language* that was almost as notable for its flaws as for its merits. Had he been more pedantic, the dictionary would have been more accurate, but it would have lost the charm that he injected by expressing his prejudices in composing definitions. In his famous definition of "oats," for example, he gave vent to his prejudice against Scotland: "a grain, which in England is generally given to horses, but in Scotland supports the people." In his definition of "Grub Street" he summed up with wry humor his feelings about his long years as an impoverished writer: "a street in London, much inhabited by writers of small histories, dictionaries, and temporary poems, whence any such production is called 'Grub Street.' " And his definition of "network" is often quoted as the kind that confuses rather than clarifies: "anything reticulated or decussated, at equal distances, with interstices between the intersections."

Seven years before the dictionary was published Johnson dedicated to Lord Chesterfield a pamphlet entitled *Plan of an English Dictionary.* Chesterfield donated ten pounds to help with this project but failed to give Johnson the kind of support he had longed for. Shortly before the dictionary was published — but at a time when its success was certain — Chesterfield published two favorable notices about the work. Johnson, furious that Chesterfield should offer praise at this point, wrote a letter that is now considered a milepost in social history. If it did not quite lead to the end of the system of patronage in literature, it did at least make all impoverished writers prouder of their craft and less willing to grovel before those who had the power to offer them financial support. A portion of that letter reads:

> Seven years, my Lord, have now passed since I waited in your outward rooms or was repulsed from your door, during which time I have been pushing on my work through difficul-

ties of which it is useless to complain, and have brought it at last to the verge of publication without one act of assistance, one word of encouragement or one smile of favour. Such treatment I did not expect, for I never had a patron before.

. . . Is not a patron, my Lord, one who looks with unconcern on a man struggling for life in the water and, when he has reached ground, encumbers him with help? The notice which you have been pleased to take of my labors, had it been early, had been kind; but it has been delayed till I am indifferent and cannot enjoy it, till I am solitary and cannot impart it, till I am known and do not want it.

I hope it is no very cynical asperity not to confess obligation where no benefits have been received, or to be unwilling that the public should consider me as owing that to a patron, which providence has enabled me to do for myself. Having carried on my work thus far with so little obligation to any favourer of learning, I shall not be disappointed though I should conclude it, if less be possible, with less, for I have been long wakened from that dream of hope, in which I once boosted myself with such exaltation, My Lord, Your Lordship's most humble, most obedient servant.

Sam Johnson

Johnson probably wept while composing that letter, especially when he inscribed the phrase "till I am solitary and cannot impart it," for he was referring to the death of his beloved wife while he was laboring on the dictionary and while he still had a monumental amount of work to do. With the cadences of that letter lingering in the mind and with an awareness that it was written by a man exhausted from years of toil, the reader has little inclination to sympathize with Lord Chesterfield. Chesterfield didn't, in fact, deserve a rebuke as stinging as the one delivered by Johnson. He had written the favorable notices about the dictionary only because he was urged to do so by the bookseller Dodsley. To Chesterfield's credit it should be noted that he was favorably impressed by the writing skill Johnson demonstrated in the letter, and said, "This man has great power." And Chesterfield told Dodsley that he "would have turned off the best servant he ever had, if he had known that he denied him to a man who would have always been more than welcome."

No better specimen of a Grub Street writer could be found than Burke's fellow student at Trinity College, Oliver Goldsmith. In 1758 Goldsmith wrote an unsigned flattering review of Burke's *Sublime and Beautiful*. Burke liked the review — naturally! — and managed to find out who wrote it. One day he met Goldsmith at the shop of Robert Dodsley, the bookseller, and they resumed their acquaintanceship.

Goldsmith's life up to this point had been marked with tragicomic failure. He didn't know what to do with himself after he got his degree from Trinity, but his family was pressuring him to become a professional man and thus bring credit to them. So he sampled one profession after another. Within a few years he was a clergyman, a teacher, a lawyer, a physician. He wasn't much good at any of these professions. For a time he wandered about Europe, playing a flute to earn his meals and a bed for the night. He attended lectures at universities in several countries, picking up a hodgepodge of miscellaneous knowledge. Without deliberately preparing for the profession of writing, he was storing up experiences that would one day find expression in delightful plays, poems, and novels.

In 1756 he arrived in London with empty pockets. By taking hack writing assignments he managed to support himself. But as soon as he got paid for a piece he would stuff himself with rich food or buy a piece of silly finery. Those years when he was forced to wear the ludicrous garb of a sizar had left deep wounds on his psyche. Now, whenever he heard the lovely sound of coins jingling in his pockets, he would trot off to the tailor's, gaze with a feverish light in his eyes at samples of fancy fabrics, and order an outfit that would make people sit up and take notice. By the time the bills came in, he would be broke again. No matter how much hack writing he did, he never caught up with his debts.

He longed desperately for admiration, but seldom got it. So he was ecstatic when Edmund Burke made overtures of friendship. Burke had by this time made something of a reputation and acquired the kind of friends whom Goldsmith regarded with awe. To be invited to Burke's home for dinner, to have Burke introduce him to persons like David Garrick and Samuel Johnson was so delightful that Goldsmith went around bragging about his famous friends. He was more of a Somebody than people realized. If he now put on silly airs, we should be indulgent with him. After all, he had not been one of those Trinity College students who were invited to the palatial homes of Dublin.

Now he was even sometimes inviting famous people to his home. One evening Goldsmith gave a supper at his place for two guests — the Reverend Thomas Percy, editor of a notable collection of ancient English poetry, and Samuel Johnson. On the way to Goldsmith's Percy stopped to pick up Johnson at his home. He was startled to find Johnson wearing a scarlet waistcoat and a hat glorified with gold lace, also a freshly powdered, brand-new wig. When Percy asked Johnson why he was dressed so handsomely, Johnson replied, "Why, Sir, I hear that Goldsmith, who is a very great sloven, justifies his disregard for cleanliness and decency by quoting my practice; and I am desirous this night to show him a better example."

But Johnson's feeling for Goldsmith is better indicated by his deeds than by his words. Once, in 1762, Goldsmith was in such desperate financial straits that his landlady threatened to have him arrested for not paying his rent. Goldsmith sent an urgent note to Johnson. Johnson made a practice of staying in bed until noon and starting the day by leisurely drinking huge quantities of tea. But that morning he gave the messenger a guinea to pass on to Goldsmith, then flung on some clothes and hurried over to his place. Johnson described the scene as follows:

I perceived that he had already changed my guinea, and had got a bottle of Madeira and a glass before him. I put the cork into the bottle, desired he would be calm, and began to talk to him of the means by which he might be extricated. He then told me that he had a novel ready for the press, which he produced to me. I looked into it, and saw its merit; told the landlady I should soon return, and having gone to a bookseller, sold it for sixty pounds.

For generations to come, secondary-school students in English-speaking countries would be reading that novel, which was entitled *The Vicar of Wakefield*. But the bookseller who gave Johnson the sixty pounds didn't think much of the manuscript and bought it only because of Johnson's recommendation. The book remained unpublished until Goldsmith had begun to make a name for himself as a playwright.

Burke, who seemed rich to Goldsmith, did not regard himself as at all well off. In fact, he needed a much larger income now that he had two sons, much more than he was earning as editor of the *Annual Register*. He started to look for ways to supplement his income.

In 1759 he met William Gerard Hamilton, a wealthy young man who shared Burke's interests in literature and politics. Hamilton was nicknamed "Single-Speech Hamilton" because he began his career in Parliament with a brilliant speech, then hardly ever rose to speak again. The speech, which lasted from two o'clock in the afternoon to two o'clock next morning, was said to have been composed by Samuel Johnson, who had been a friend of Hamilton's for a long time. Hamilton was handsome and clever and had some talent for writing, but he could not speak extemporaneously. In a debate, where he would have to think rapidly, he was at a total loss. Perceiving that Burke's talents could be useful to him, Hamilton offered the young Irishman the position of secretary-companion. Burke was delighted to accept. He assumed that the position would offer him financial security and still allow him time to work on his own literary projects.

When the Earl of Halifax became Lord-Lieutenant of Ireland in 1761, he chose Hamilton as his Chief Secretary, and Hamilton asked Burke to accompany him to Ireland. Burke was overjoyed. Now he could visit his parents and his old friends and see the places that had been dear to him. Because of his Irish background, he could be of special service to Hamilton. Another pleasing factor of this arrangement — from Hamilton's viewpoint — was that he wouldn't have to pay Burke out of his own pocket. He got Burke a pension of three hundred pounds a year from the Irish Parliament. Since the Irish Parliament met only in the winter of every other year, Burke could spend most of his time in London. For a time it seemed like an ideal arrangement.

In August, 1761, with his wife and children, Burke arrived in Dublin well before the opening of the Irish Parliament, in time for long visits with his parents and old friends.

It was good that he could be in Ireland at that time, for his father died a few months later, and Burke was present at his deathbed. The elder Burke's will, after providing for his wife and daughter, divided the rest of the estate among the three sons, Garrett, Edmund, and Richard. There were legacies of twenty pounds each for Edmund's two little boys. Since he was the only one of the three brothers who ever married, his sons were the only ones who would carry on the family name.

Shortly after the death of the elder Burke, little Christopher died. Now little Richard was the only member of the younger generation left to carry on the family name. The bereaved parents lavished all their affection on him, to the point of spoiling him.

Since Burke was now spending most of his time in London, he continued to strengthen his friendships there. In February, 1764, he was chosen as a charter member of a club founded by Samuel Johnson and the artist Joshua Reynolds. Burke proposed his father-in-law as a member, and Johnson and Reynolds readily agreed. Dr. Nugent, well-read, broad-minded, and gentle-mannered, met Johnson's requirement that all members must be "clubbable." Noll Goldsmith, too, was selected. His touching combination of knowledge and ignorance, artlessness and design, delicacy and grossness endeared him to the founders of the club. Johnson and Goldsmith had had a bit of difficulty in adjusting to each other after their first meeting because Goldsmith's conversation was often silly. But before long they were drawn to each other by the fact that both of them had suffered the sneers of fools and the pangs of grinding poverty. And Reynolds was Goldsmith's closest friend.

Reynolds was England's greatest portrait painter of the period, a man who had grown wealthy in the practice of his profession, but who enjoyed the company of creative spirits more than that of other men of wealth. As a result of a bad cold he caught while copying Raphael in the damp, chilly air of the Vatican, he had become deaf and had to use an ear trumpet. But with that ear trumpet he managed to pick up everything he wanted to hear. His face was rather disfigured from smallpox scars, and his upper lip was slightly defective. Yet he was attractive. He dressed with unostentatious elegance, and his manners were gentle. Despite his great respect for Johnson, he was at times disturbed by Johnson's uncouthness. And much as he enjoyed Johnson's brilliant conversation, he was sharp enough to observe that Johnson sometimes tried to turn the most light and airy dispute into a ferocious gladiatorial duel. Johnson, despite his friendly feelings for Reynolds, was a bit annoyed — as were some others — that Reynolds often seemed a bit too good to be true. The fact that he had no enemies made him a rare specimen in eighteenth-century London. Johnson once said of him, "Sir Joshua Reynolds possesses the largest store of inoffensiveness of any man that I know."

One famous Londoner was strangely among the missing when the charter members of the club were chosen — actor

David Garrick. He was a good friend of the other members. In fact, he had known Johnson since boyhood, and Johnson had been his teacher. In 1737 the two of them arrived in London with a total of fourpence in their combined pockets — at any rate, that is the story they liked to tell in later years. They may have had a bit more, but the precise amount doesn't matter. They were, in fact, desperately poor. But Garrick's experience with poverty was brief. While he was quite young, he inherited enough money to be able to indulge in his passion for acting. Without going through a period of struggle, he shot to the heights of his profession. Maybe the ease with which he attained success explained his insufferable conceit. Offstage as well as onstage, he was always seeking applause, always trying to control his audience by his skill with gesture and voice modulation. His conversation was intelligent, far more intelligent than Goldsmith's, for example.

But all those qualities that might have made him a welcome addition to the club were overshadowed by his smug assumption that he couldn't conceivably be ignored when the club members were selected. When he learned about the club, he told Reynolds, "I like it much. I think I shall be of you." Reynolds relayed this remark to Johnson, who roared, *"He'll be of us!* How does he know we will *permit* him? The first duke in England has no right to use such language!" Garrick would pay a dear price for that offhand remark. Not until he had gone through a chastening period of nine years was he eventually allowed to join the club.

Yet, if Johnson seems to have been unduly harsh in this punishment of Garrick, he always remained fiercely loyal to Garrick. Nobody dared utter a word against Garrick when Johnson was present. Johnson couldn't forget that David and his father had been among the few who befriended him during his years of youthful poverty.

The members met every Monday evening at a Soho coffeehouse called the Turk's Head. At first their conversation centered on literature, and outsiders referred to the group as "The Literary Club." But its members never called it anything more specific than the Club. And they did not confine their talk to literature. Any topic that made for good conversation was suitable, although the topic usually had something to do with writing. Before long the influence of the Club became formidable. If they liked a new book, an entire edition might be sold out in one day. If they didn't like it, its chances of success were limited.

All the club members were male. But that was not because eighteenth-century London lacked women who could hold their own in literary conversations. There was, in fact, a coterie of brilliant women known as "the blue-stockings." The originator of the bluestocking society was a witty Irishwoman named Elizabeth Vesey, wife of Agmondesham Vesey, member of the Irish Parliament. During her annual visit to Bath she chanced to meet Benjamin Stillingfleet, an impoverished botanist-poet, and impulsively invited him to one of her "conversations" (social gatherings where the literary and fashionable worlds were united). Stillingfleet protested he had no suitable clothes to wear at such a gathering. Mrs. Vesey glanced down at his blue worsted stockings and said airily, "Don't mind dress. Come in your blue stockings." When Stillingfleet showed up, he found the ladies wearing "night gowns" of brocade and lutestring and the men outshining the women in sartorial splendor.

Stillingfleet sized up the group and said, with a rueful smile, "Don't mind dress. Come in your blue stockings."

The other guests were delighted. They welcomed him to their group and gave him the affectionate nickname "blue stockings," which in time would become the name assigned to the entire group.

Another prominent member of the group was Mrs. Elizabeth Carter, who had been a friend of Samuel Johnson's since he was in his twenties. She had a scholarly command of several ancient as well as several modern languages. Johnson was particularly impressed at the way this woman associated freely with Grub Street writers and could whip up a pudding as skillfully as she could handle a Greek translation. Johnson considered her one of the best Greek scholars he had ever known.

The member of the bluestockings who won the most lasting fame was Hannah More, who would in her later years become a philanthropist and a social reformer. When she first joined the bluestockings, however, she was still in her twenties, and her interests were primarily literary. She became the chief chronicler and poet laureate of the blues. The first time she met Johnson, at the home of Joshua Reynolds, Reynolds warned her that she might find Johnson in a sad mood. But when she walked up the stairs to meet the great man, he advanced to meet her "with good humour in his countenance and a macaw of Sir Joshua's in his hand," while he gallantly greeted her with a verse from a hymn that she had composed. She met Burke in May, 1771, and described him as "the sublime and beautiful Edmund Burke."

But the "Queen of the Blues" was a strikingly beautiful woman named Elizabeth Montagu, born to great wealth and the wife of a wealthy man. She was so brilliant that she had been considered an infant prodigy. By the time she was thirteen, she had started to find fashionable social gatherings insufferably dull. On a visit to Bath she was so repelled with the way the wealthy idled away their hours that she wrote in a letter, " 'How d'ye do?' is all one hears in the morning and 'What's trump?' in the afternoon." As a grown woman she couldn't abide trivial pastimes. From eleven in the morning until eleven at night her "Chinese" room was filled with a succession of the brightest and (intellectually) best. Her guests were not allowed to play cards, indulge in scandalous gossip, or discuss politics. "Common or genteel swearing" wasn't countenanced. And no alcoholic beverages were served. Johnson said of her: "That lady expects more mind in conversation than any person I ever met with . . . she displays such powers of ratiocination . . . as are amazing."

The one requirement for an invitation to her home was that the guest must be a lively conversationalist. When she read Burke's *Sublime and Beautiful,* she was so enthusiastic about it that she invited him to her house. Thereafter, he and his wife were frequent guests at the gatherings of the bluestockings.

Mrs. Montagu was delighted when the Club was formed. She was personally acquainted with its members and keenly interested in reports of what went on at its meetings.

Burke's patron, William Gerard Hamilton, was typical of the kind of person who would have been welcomed neither at Mrs. Montagu's home nor at the Club. His wealth and good looks were not enough to make him acceptable in such exclusive circles. And his literary ability was negligible. He was essentially a brainpicker, who exploited the talents of others to advance his own interests. The longer Burke worked for him the more evident it became that Hamilton assumed he had bought Burke's brains. After six years Burke had had his fill. He had a violent quarrel with Hamilton, with each of them hurling insults at the other. Hamilton nastily reminded Burke of the pension of three hundred pounds a year from the Irish Parliament. Legally, Burke had a right to retain that pension even after leaving Hamilton's employ, but he was so angry that he said he didn't want the pension or anything else associated with Hamilton. Seething with indignation over Hamilton's behavior, Burke dashed off letter after letter, telling his friends what Hamilton had said and done. The essence of the story is contained in a passage from one of those letters:

> Six of the best years of my life he took me from every pursuit of literary reputation, or of improvement of my fortune. In that time he made his own fortune (a very great one) and he has also taken to himself the very little one which I have made. In all this time you may easily conceive, how much I felt at seeing myself left behind by almost all my contemporaries. There

never was a season more favourable for any man who chose to enter into the Career of publick Life; and I think I am not guilty of Ostentation in supposing my own Moral Character and my industry, many friends and connections, when Mr. H. sought my acquaintance were not at all inferior to those of several, whose fortune is at this day upon a very different footing from mine.

Burke's indignation is understandable. He had at least as much jealousy in his makeup as most men. It was galling to see himself outstripped by men of lesser talents. He had reached the age of thirty-six without achieving half of what he had hoped to accomplish. But if anything can be said in Hamilton's defense, it is that there was never a clear understanding about what sort of service he was entitled to as Burke's employer. Their original arrangement was rather vague. Hamilton may have behaved no worse than other eighteenth-century patrons in believing that writers should grovel for whatever crumbs were thrown their way.

But Burke's angry letters show him in a far less favorable light than does Johnson's exquisitely phrased letter to Chesterfield. Burke's letters often reveal an unpleasant trait — his tendency to resort to name-calling when angry. In later years he would frequently reveal this trait. Granted that Hamilton's behavior was less than admirable, Burke himself was even less admirable when he described Hamilton as "a sullen, vain, proud, selfish, canker-hearted envious reptile," "an infamous scoundrel," "the most consummate villain that ever lived."

While still in Hamilton's employ Burke continued to write for the *Annual Register*. In 1765 he wrote several pieces about the American situation. The Americans had violently objected to the Stamp Act, which imposed taxes on fifty-five articles in common use in the colonies. From the British viewpoint, the act seemed to be reasonable. The colonists had benefited from England's Seven Years' War with France. English blood had been shed in that war. English victory meant that the predominantly Protestant Americans were spared the persecution they would have suffered as subjects of the Catholic monarch, King Louis XV of France. The war had been so costly that taxes were now needed to pay off the debt. In all fairness, as Burke saw it, Americans should help to pay that debt and not expect the English to bear the entire burden.

The Americans didn't see it that way. When they learned about the Stamp Act, they did everything they could to keep it from being enforced. They destroyed property, threatened stamp agents, delivered fiery sermons, wrote impassioned pamphlets. And they refused to buy goods manufactured in England. The word "boycott" was not yet in use — the Americans referred to the practice as "non-importation." Whatever it was called, it was effective. It hurt Englishmen where they would feel it most, in their pocketbooks.

Burke was basically sympathetic with the Americans. He thought that the Stamp Act was ill-considered, whatever justification there might be for it. The Americans didn't object to taxation as such. What they minded was the high-handed way in which the tax had been thrust on them. Had they been allowed to vote, in their own assemblies, for funds to help pay the war debt, they might have been generous in voting funds. Burke felt that Americans deserved to be treated with respect and with recognition for the fact that they, too, had shed their blood in the recent war. But he did not agree with some of the arguments that the Americans used in opposing the Stamp Act. Their charge of "taxation without representation," he felt, lacked validity. There were practical reasons why Americans should not be represented in Parliament: the long time that it took to travel from America to London and back, and the fact that Americans were no worse off than most Englishmen so far as representation was concerned. Some large English cities had no representatives in Parliament. Some rotten boroughs (communities where the population had dwindled to few residents or none at all) did have representatives. And many of the seats in Parliament were held by representatives of pocket boroughs, which were controlled by a single family. The notion that people should be represented in accordance with their numbers was foreign to Burke. Parliament took care of the interests of all British subjects, including Americans. But his strongest argument against American representation was that many Americans owned slaves and were therefore unfit to sit in a parliament of free men.

The "interests" represented in Parliament were those related to the land, commerce, the armed forces, the civil service, and the Church of England. The fact that a man possessed property was taken as evidence that he had enjoyed at least a modicum of education and therefore had the ability to think intelligently about issues that might affect the nation's prosperity. Those who were denied the right to vote for representatives because they owned no property did enjoy the privilege of knowing that they were "virtually" represented in Parliament, for what that might be worth. In Burke's day anyone who believed that the propertyless should have any say in the making of the nation's laws would have been considered "radical."

The voteless mob did not accept this situation passively. Eighteenth-century elections were often marked by violence, with most of that violence provoked by the voteless. They often assaulted the electors, waylaid them on the roads leading to the polls, or cooped them up in a drunken stupor until the election was over. They resorted to threats that may have had some effect on the way certain electors might vote. (The secret ballot was still a century away.) In one way or another the common people did have at least a little say about who would be seated in Parliament, but the tactics they used simply served to show how dangerous they might be if they should be granted the right to vote.

Burke did not remain out of work very long after his quarrel with Hamilton. With the support of Will Burke, he got a much better job as secretary to the new Prime Minister, the Marquess of Rockingham. Rockingham, a year younger than Burke, was the center of a group of politicians who had opposed the American policies of King George III. He was enormously wealthy and had acquired a cosmopolitan background by years of travel. More important, he was a man of high principles. To be appointed his secretary was a big step up for Burke.

The Duke of Newcastle was furious at Rockingham for choosing an Irish nobody for such an important position. Hoping that Rockingham would replace Burke with a man of Newcastle's choice, Newcastle now told Rockingham that Burke was a Papist, educated by Jesuits. Since anti-Catholic sentiment was strong, such a charge could damage both Burke and Rockingham. But Rockingham was not the man to listen to one side of a story. He asked Burke what he had to say for himself. Burke said that he did have many Catholic relatives, but he himself had always been a member of the Established Church. He offered to resign rather than cause Rockingham embarrassment, but Rockingham refused to accept his resignation.

Rumors about Burke's religious background continued to circulate. For the rest of his life he would be caricatured as a tall, thin, waspish figure with a beaked nose, wearing the cassock and biretta of the Jesuits.

Burke was Rockingham's secretary for only a few months. In December, 1765, through the influence of a friend of Will Burke's, he was elected a Member of Parliament, representing the pocket borough of Wendover. Will could have taken that seat himself, but he preferred to offer it to Edmund. Edmund would never forget that he owed his start in politics to Will.

6. Stamp 'Act Speeches "Fill the Town With Wonder" (1766)

By THIS TIME Burke had paid many visits to the House of Commons. At the age of twenty-one, as an Irish greenhorn, he had been impressed by the "explosions of eloquence" from the speakers. After he had learned more about British politics, he listened to debates with more concern for the content of the speeches than for the theatrical displays indulged in by some of the speakers. He became less inclined to give the speaker credit for felicitous turns of phrase after he learned that the speech might have been composed by some obscure hack writer and merely memorized by the speaker. The kind of speech that Burke found most impressive was the kind delivered by someone who knew what he was talking about, someone who could speak brilliantly even under the pressures of a heated debate.

When Burke became editor of the *Annual Register* in 1758, he was twenty-nine years old and had acquired quite a fund of knowledge of British politics. As he watched proceedings in the House of Commons, taking notes for articles, he became more critical and more disgusted with the lackadaisical attitude of those members who felt no concern for their obligations as legislators. Such men could be dangerous to a country. They enjoyed the prestige of being

Members of Parliament, but they cared nothing about the effect of laws on the welfare of their countrymen. Sometimes Burke would leave the gallery of the House of Commons with a feeling of frustration at being unable to do anything more effective than express disgust in an article for the *Annual Register*.

Had it ever occurred to him, during his years as a reporter, that he might one day become a Member of Parliament himself? Probably not. Getting a seat in Parliament was easy, all too easy, for those with great wealth and influential family connections. For those who lacked such advantages, it wasn't impossible to be elected, but they had to have the aid of someone with a parliamentary seat at his disposal. Probably Burke did not realize, until shortly before he was elected, that he would one day walk into the House of Commons as a member rather than as a mere spectator.

As he took his seat on January 14, 1766, he nodded at some members with whom he was acquainted. But most of the members did not know him and didn't seem at all interested in knowing him. They sat cracking nuts, peeling oranges, exchanging pleasantries with each other as if they were there for purely social reasons.

The House of Commons met in a surprisingly small chamber, no larger than the reception hall in the houses of some of its members. It had formerly been St. Stephen's Chapel, but all Anglican religious trappings were removed during the civil war a century ago. Now the room looked more like a simple Lutheran church. Its rows of benches could not accommodate all of its several hundred members at one time. But the problem of sufficient room rarely arose. Many members showed up only now and then. They preferred to stay on their estates, fox-hunting, enjoying their lavish gardens, wining and dining their friends and relatives. To them Parliament was a kind of club. They showed up only when they happened to be in town with nothing more amusing to do or when the king ordered them to be present to vote as he directed. Even this day, when the matter under consideration was of more than ordinary importance, there were vacant seats.

The matter under consideration was the Stamp Act. Something had to be done about it. Exactly what should be done was the topic of debate. Burke listened attentively. No more than a handful of those sitting there then knew as much about America as he did. Nobody felt more keenly that the Stamp Act had been passed without careful consideration and that it should be repealed. From the moment he took his seat he was in a state of tension as he waited for a chance to plunge into the debate. He sighed in exasperation as he listened to some of the debaters ridiculing Americans. He wanted to shout them down, but he couldn't speak until he was recognized by the Speaker. And many others were trying to get the Speaker's attention.

Even more annoying than those who ridiculed Americans were those who assumed a bored air. These members belonged to a group known as the "King's Friends," men whose seats had been bought by King George III in various ways. He had paid their campaign expenses, tempted them with offers of sinecures, pensions, military commissions. Sometimes he had offered them large sums of money. All they had to do in return was to be present whenever he so directed and to vote the way he wanted them to vote.

The King's Friends tended to look a bit like the king himself. Typically, they had corpulent builds, protruding eyes, jowly cheeks, and a manner of speaking as if they had plums in their mouths. From time to time they placed their hands daintily before their lips as they signified their boredom with a yawn. Only when the vote was taken did they spring into action. Meanwhile they had little to contribute.

Their air of unconcern irritated Burke. When the time came for him to speak, those fishy eyes would be focused upon him in contempt, and he could not be indifferent to the contempt even of those whom he held in contempt. What sort of impression would he make in his first speech?

Would he become so embarrassed that he would forget what he had intended to say? Worse still, would he become so wrought up that he would explode? Dignity was expected of him, at least in his maiden speech, and he wasn't sure that he could remain dignified once he started talking about the Stamp Act. He didn't want to get off to a bad start in Parliament. A maiden speech could be important. If he spoke brilliantly, regardless of which side of a question he supported, his audience would be delighted. Since he would probably remain in Parliament for many years, he would be welcome as one who could keep the sessions lively. But if he turned out to be a bore and a stammerer, he was doomed. Members would make no effort to conceal their disgust. They might try to drown him out by stomping their feet or simply walk ostentatiously out of the room. Sometimes, even while a good speaker was addressing the group, some member would get up, pause in front of the Speaker to bow, like a schoolboy asking his master's permission to leave the room, and walk out.

Still, it would be misleading to give the impression that the House of Commons was composed entirely, or even largely, of fops and dandies. Visitors to the House were sometimes surprised at the extreme youth of some members, but the proportion of men over sixty wasn't much smaller than the proportion who were under thirty. Eighteenth-century M.P.'s held their seats much longer than their twentieth-century counterparts. Some were army or navy officers who had seen service in America during the Seven Years' War and who were therefore familiar with Americans. Some were merchants who had been to America for reasons of business. A few were native Americans who had settled in England. But familiarity with Americans didn't necessarily make those M.P.'s feel friendly toward the Americans; with some, the reverse might be true.

Burke had ample cause to suffer from stage fright that day. Most of the members of the House of Commons had known each other for years. They knew all that was worth knowing about each other: the skeletons in family closets, the ancestry, the sources of wealth. They gossiped over each other's idiosyncrasies and misdemeanors in drawing rooms. And they could be brutally frank in the things they said about each other in letters and diaries.

There was an air of disorderliness about the room, little groups of men carrying on private conversations.

But suddenly the atmosphere changed to one of awed silence. William Pitt, former Prime Minister, had entered the room. His legs were swathed in flannel bandages. He walked as if each step caused him pain. But his figure was tall and portly, and his eyes had a gleam that aroused a chill of suspense in the spectators. Nobody had expected him to be here today. It was more than five years since he had retired to his country estate, suffering severely from gout. But he had been keeping in touch with what was going on in Parliament during his absence. Now, ill though he was, he was determined to have his say about the Stamp Act.

When he started to speak, his voice was calm and his words were moderate. He gave no clear indication of whether he thought the Stamp Act should be repealed. But everyone knew that he had long been a friend of the Americans, that the Americans considered him a hero. They had erected statues in his honor. They had named the town of Pittsburgh, Pennsylvania, after him. They drank his toast in taverns. But that was before the Stamp Act was passed. Now he knew how atrociously the Americans had behaved in reaction to the Stamp Act. What did he think of his fine American friends now?

His audience did not have to wait long to find out. His voice grew stronger and rose to a shout: "The Americans are the sons, not the bastards of England! I rejoice that America has resisted! Three millions of people so dead to all the feelings of liberty as voluntarily to submit to be slaves would have been fit instruments to have made slaves of the rest."

(The population of the colonies was actually only about two million at that time, but increasing at a rate that alarmed some Englishmen.)

Burke's eyes sparkled with delight as he joined Pitt's admirers in calling out: "Hear him!" It was the kind of speech he would have liked to deliver himself. But it would have been unthinkable for a new member to hold the floor for three hours, as Pitt now did. And to use language so deliberately offensive to those who had supported the Stamp Act.

The gist of Pitt's speech was: Taxation is no part of governing power. Parliament has no right under nature or the British constitution to tax an unrepresented people. The doctrine of "virtual" representation is a fiction. But Parliament, as the supreme governing body and legislative power, does possess authority over every other matter, and if its power to regulate trade and manufacturers should be denied, Pitt would not permit the colonies "to manufacture a lock of wool or a horseshoe or a hobnail."

Burke couldn't manage to break into the debate that day. His opportunity did not come until three days later, when he stood up to read a petition from the merchants of Manchester.

One of the strongest objections to the Stamp Act was that the American policy of nonimportation had ruined British trade. Merchants, manufacturers, shippers, and tradesmen had been suffering from a postwar depression even before the Stamp Act was passed. When the Americans stopped sending orders, hundreds of thousands of workers lost their jobs. The unemployed men were threatening to march on Parliament. Businessmen in all leading English cities had sent petitions to the House of Commons, urging repeal of the Stamp Act. All Burke had to do was to read one such petition and he would have chalked up his maiden speech in Parliament.

But once he was on his feet his pent-up emotions led him to say far more than he had intended to say. After reading the petition from Manchester, he burst into a tirade against the Stamp Act. The other members stared at him, dumbfounded. Nobody got up and walked out of the room. Nobody seemed to be making a sound. What did their silence signify? Burke knew that he was attracting great attention, but the faces looked blurred. He could not tell what was going on in the minds of his audience. Words erupted from his lips, but he seemed to have no control over those words. When he sat down, his face was flushed. What had he actually said? He couldn't remember a word. But he felt sure he had made a spectacle of himself. By nightfall he would be a laughingstock in London taverns and drawing rooms. He waited until he felt his breathing return to normal. Then he stood up awkwardly, bowed to the Speaker, and hurried out of the room. When he got home, he dashed off a letter to an old friend — Charles O'Hara, member of the Irish Parliament:

Sir William Meredith desired me to present the Manchester Petition. I know not what struck me, but I took a sudden resolution to say something about it, though I had got it but that moment, and had scarcely time to read it, short as it was. I did say something. What it was, I know not upon my honour. I felt like a man drunk. Lord Frederic Campbell made me some answer to which I replied, ill enough too. But I was by this time pretty well on my legs. I was now heated and would have been much better, but Mr. G. Savile caught the Speaker's eye before me; and it was then thought better not to proceed further, as it would keep off the business of the day. So that I ventured up again on the motion, and spoke some minutes, poorly, but not quite as ill as before. All I hoped was to plunge in and get off the first horrors. I had no hopes of making a figure.

O'Hara replied to Burke in a letter dated January 25, offering encouragement and advice:

Your voice will form from practice, your manner will improve, the great point you are to attend to is temper. Was it not Jephson that used to tell you that in some circumstances you had an air of anger? Get rid of this air.

It's a pity that nobody thought of making a shorthand record of Burke's maiden speech. But he was a new member. Nobody knew what to expect when he stood up. He himself couldn't remember what he had said. That it was a remarkable speech we know from what others said of it.

David Garrick was sitting in the visitors' gallery while Burke was speaking. That evening Garrick sent a note to Burke:

> I had the honour and pleasure of enjoying your virgin eloquence! I most sincerely congratulate you upon it — I am very nice and very hard to please and where my friends are concerned most hypercritical. I pronounce that you will answer the warmest wishes of your warmest friend. I was much pleased.

Horace Walpole, son of former Prime Minister Robert Walpole and a writer of considerable repute, noted in his diary:

> There appeared in this debate a new speaker, whose fame for eloquence soon rose high above the ordinary pitch. His name was Edmund Burke . . . an Irishman, of a Roman Catholic family, and actually married to one of that persuasion. He had been known to the public for a few years by his "Essay on the Sublime and Beautiful," and other ingenious works; but the narrowness of his fortune had kept him down, and his best revenue had arisen from writing for booksellers.

In a later speech in the House of Commons, William Pitt paid tribute to Burke's first speech. Samuel Johnson said that Burke had "filled the town with wonder. Burke is a great man by nature, and is expected to achieve civil greatness."

Bluestocking Mrs. Elizabeth Montagu went to hear Burke speak on the final day of the Stamp Act debates. She wrote to a friend: "Our friend Mr. Burke spoke divinely, yes divinely, don't misunderstand me, and report he spoke as well as mortal man can do, I tell you he spoke better."

After hearing such comments, Burke recovered his confidence in his ability to hold his own on the floor of the House of Commons. Never again would he feel shaky about speaking his mind there.

The debate on the repeal of the Stamp Act lasted several weeks. Those opposed to repeal strenuously objected to any change in colonial policy. The king could not be expected to yield to colonial insolence. Repeal would be humiliating to him and those who had approved the act. Some opponents went so far as to suggest that they would "butcher all America" rather than give up the Stamp Act. They wanted to tear up colonial charters, abolish colonial legislatures, dispatch a fleet and an army to cram the stamps down the colonists' throats. One speaker said that William Pitt ought to be sent to the Tower for praising American resistance. Another accused Pitt of sacrificing the rights of the mother country "to the pitiful ambition of obtaining an huzza from the American rioters."

But eventually — at one-thirty on the morning of February 22, 1766 — the House of Commons voted, 275-167, to repeal the Stamp Act. How much influence did Burke's oratory have on this vote? Probably none. Much as the other members may have admired his speeches, his words counted far less than Pitt's. Possibly the most effective speech in favor of repeal was one delivered by a man who wasn't even a member of the House of Commons — Benjamin Franklin, agent for several American colonies. He knew, better than anyone in his audience, how to present the American side of the story.

Yet the influence that outweighed all others was pressure applied by British businessmen. They made it clear that the entire nation would suffer keenly unless trade with America was quickly resumed. On March 18, 1766, King George reluctantly signed the act repealing the Stamp Act.

When word of the repeal reached America, bells rang joyously, and bonfires burned on hilltops. The imperial flag was unfurled, and toasts were drunk to the health of King George III. On the whole, the celebrations were orderly, with no more drunkenness than might reasonably be expected when toasts to King George were followed by toasts to William Pitt, Edmund Burke, and others who had favored repeal.

Repeal of the Stamp Act was also a cause for rejoicing in England. One British cartoon, published shortly after the repeal, showed the author of the Stamp Act, George Grenville, carrying the coffin of his dead brainchild to the "Family Vault." In the background of this cartoon is a warehouse bearing a sign with the legend "Goods NOW Ship'd for America."

In their excitement, most of the celebrants overlooked one important detail, and that was that Parliament still insisted on its right to tax the colonies when and as it pleased. The act repealing the Stamp Act was accompanied by a Declaratory Act designed to affirm Parliament's right to tax the colonies. Burke, who believed that Parliament indeed had such a right but should use it discreetly, was one of those who voted in favor of the Declaratory Act.

7. Edmund Burke, M.P., Man of Property
(1768 . . .)

BURKE WORKED LIKE fury during his first few months as a Member of Parliament. Many years later, describing that period in his life, he said that he came close to death because he had worked so hard at that time.

Yet men often work hard in the service of their country without driving themselves to the brink of death. Why did Burke work so hard? It could be that he had come to love the British Empire so dearly that he was willing to give his life, if need be, to preserve that empire. He now thought of himself as an Englishman who happened to be born in Ireland, rather than as an Irishman who happened to be living in England. And he undoubtedly did care intensely about the British Empire and about his obligations as a Member of Parliament.

But his tendency to overwork — a tendency he would have all his life — had a more personal basis. He may have worked unduly hard in 1766 because he wanted to make up for the precious years that he had wasted while working for William Gerard Hamilton. Burke was thirty-seven when he entered Parliament, a rather advanced age for a man about to embark upon a parliamentary career. Since many members got their seats through family influence, they usually entered Parliament when they were about twenty-one.

And it was not uncommon for men to be appointed to Cabinet posts before the age of thirty.

Besides, it must be remembered that Burke received no pay for his work in Parliament — and he had a family to support. Most of the other members were independently wealthy or received financial aid from the king. Burke was far too conscientious to neglect his parliamentary duties; yet he had to have some lucrative employment. In addition to the hours he spent in the House of Commons or preparing his speeches, he continued working for the *Annual Register*. Since parliamentary sessions sometimes lasted into the small hours of the morning, he undoubtedly arrived home many nights in a state of exhaustion, then got up early next morning to prepare a speech for a forthcoming debate. And it was quite a physical strain to deliver a speech. The speaker remained standing all the while he was talking (in fact, the common way of referring to a speaker was to say that he was "on his legs"). And Burke's speeches often lasted for two or three hours.

What did it mean to be the wife of such a busy man? Jane's contribution to her husband's work was unobtrusive, but visitors to their home were impressed with her quiet efficiency. Sometimes, while talking with guests, Burke would refer to some book or paper, and Jane would quickly produce it. Keeping Burke's records in order, making sure that he always had an ample supply of pens and ink and fresh paper couldn't have been easy, since he wrote at white heat and left to her the job of tidying up. In every way she could she tried to save his energies, playing the part of both secretary and wife — with no financial compensation, of course. Perhaps she needed a vacation as much as he did by the summer of 1766.

Lord Inchiquin, who later became a neighbor of the Burkes, wrote an amusingly frank description of how Burke depended on his wife's secretarial services:

> In His House Burke is quiet if not contradicted in anything; but walks about it heedless of every concern — knowing nothing

of Servants, — expenses, &c, &c, — He is very careless of his papers, — would drop on the floor a paper though it contained treason as He would a newspaper cover. — Mrs. Burke watches over everything, — collects His scraps, arranges & dockets every paper, — My Dear Jane will Burke say, I want such a paper, — it is produced — as conversation proceeds He calls for others. She produces them — He asks for one which she cannot remember. Yes, Yes, Yes, my dear Jane, — no contradiction, it must be found. — She examines.

Yet the vacation the Burkes took in Ireland in August, 1766, was not a pleasure trip. One reason why they went to Ireland at that time was that Burke's brother Garrett had died in 1765, and Burke had to settle the estate. As eldest male in the Burke family, Garrett had been responsible for taking care of his mother's Catholic relatives. Now that responsibility fell on Edmund's shoulders, and it turned out to be an expensive and time-consuming responsibility. The Nagles, as we know, lived in greater comfort than most Catholics. Although they weren't allowed to own land, they lived almost as well as if they did own land, and paid rent to Burke. Legally, he had the right to press them for overdue rents, to raise their rents, even to evict them. But it was unthinkable that he would do such a thing to relatives with whom he had spent happy childhood years. He inherited something from Garrett, and he made some income from rents, but those gains were offset by the fact that some of his relatives now became a financial burden. He and Jane were often asked to be godparents, and that meant a costly gift for each newborn and more than a token interest in the child's future. For the rest of his life Burke would send books and other presents to his godchildren and help them to make their way in the world. Later, when he had acquired property in England, his Irish relatives would come to visit him, sometimes remaining for months or even years.

This 1766 visit to Ireland was busy for other reasons, too. Burke's achievements in the House of Commons had been widely reported in Ireland, and he was showered with the honors usually bestowed on the local boy who makes good. He received more invitations to banquets than he could possibly accept. At those banquets he did attend he was expected to speak — everyone wanted a sample of the Burke eloquence.

He spent some time at Ballyduff and at Loughrea, where his mother and sister Juliana were now living, and the gentlemen and ladies of the area, including old childhood friends, flocked to call on him.

At Ballitore, where Richard Shackleton had taken his father's place as headmaster, Jane created a sensation by wearing a fancy French bonnet. But her reason for doing so casts an interesting light on her personality. On an earlier visit she had worn no head covering. Richard Shackleton's wife Elizabeth, who wore the simple clothes favored by the Quakers, adored pretty clothes on other woman. She expressed surprise that Jane wore no covering on her head. Jane remembered the remark. Next time she came to Ballitore wearing the fanciest bonnet ever seen in those parts.

Richard Shackleton's daughter Mary later wrote a description of Burke as he appeared to her at the time of this visit, when she was eight years old:

Edmund Burke was expected with impatient wonder. The chaise stopped at the big gate, which unfolded wide, and my imagination still presents the graceful form of Edmund, as I beheld him from the nursery window. . . . The plain dress of Edmund disappointed my expectation, and I thought the postillion's habit, daubed with livery lace, much more elegant; the sight of our guest's laced waistcoat, however, a little reconciled me. Yet when, in taking a survey of the family of his friend, he stood over me as I sat in a little chair, and viewed me through the glass which assisted his short sight, I felt so abashed and confused that I directly annexed the idea of austerity in his countenance; nor could the testimony of many witnesses efface that idea, till I afterwards saw him in London in the year 1784, when with a very uncommon sensation of pleasure and surprise it was at once put to flight; for never did I see so much benignity and intelligence united as in the manly beauty of that countenance in which were blended the expressions of every superior quality of the head and of the heart.

In Galway, where Burke's Norman ancestors (originally named De Burgos) had settled six centuries earlier, the bells of the city rang out in his honor, and he was presented with the freedom of the city. His mother proudly looked on as honors were bestowed on him. But a letter she sent a friend at this time reveals her as a sweet, modest woman. She had evidently seen too much of life to be thrown off-balance by the glitter of its tinselly moments:

My dear Molly, I believe you think me very vain, but as you are a Mother, I hope you will excuse it. I assure you it is not the honours that are done him that make me vain of him, but the goodness of his heart, than which I believe no man living has a better. I am sure there cannot be a better son, nor I think a better daughter in law than his wife.

What about Burke's own attitude toward the honors bestowed upon him? Did they go to his head? Evidently not — or not so much that he looked down on those of humbler station.

One day his former teacher O'Halloran came to call on him early in the morning. Holding his weatherbeaten cap in a wrinkled hand, the old hedge-schoolmaster knocked on the door of the house where Burke was staying and hesitantly told the maid that he wished to speak with Burke. O'Halloran's heart pounded as he waited. Would the famous Edmund Burke be too busy to have time for a shabby old man?

Burke was shaving at the time, but he hurried downstairs with the lather still on his face. Tears of affection filled his eyes as he took both of O'Halloran's hands in his and insisted that they must spend the entire day reminiscing about days of yore.

"And sure enough I did," O'Halloran would tell people for years afterward. "But was that all, d'you suppose? No, to be sure, it was not. Didn't he put five gold guineas into my hand as I was coming away?"

Generosity was always one of Burke's outstanding traits, and few of those who benefited from that generosity were aware that he couldn't easily afford what he gave. In 1766 his income was only a few hundred pounds a year, and a guinea was worth one shilling more than a pound.

Burke's attitude toward money was never niggardly. Since he never had to keep household accounts, he had no realistic notion of what it cost to keep food on the table and wood in the fireplace. Jane took care of such matters. She spared him the petty annoyance of planning budgets and dealing with tradesmen. And Burke never knew the strain of being the only breadwinner of a family. Living in a comfortable home, where several adult males shared expenses, he never knew the desolate experience of looking at an accumulation of bills and knowing he lacked the means to pay them. The other men in his household, believing he had far more important things to do with his time, never distracted him with arguments about money.

That may be one reason why, in 1768, he made the most foolish purchase of his life — a 600-acre estate in Beaconsfield, Buckinghamshire. Little though he knew about what it cost to run a house, he must have realized that such a place was beyond his means.

It is understandable that he should want a home of his own. In 1768 he was thirty-nine and had been married for eleven years. All that time he had lived under his father-in-law's roof. Nobody could ask for a pleasanter father-in-law than Dr. Nugent. But Burke was no different from most men in wishing to be master in his own home.

Another good reason for buying a house in the country was his health. He had never been strong. And life in eighteenth-century London imperiled the health of all who lived there unless they could escape from time to time to a country place. A plague and a great fire a century earlier had led to a few improvements in sanitation, but Londoners still knew little about social hygiene. Open sewers ran through many thoroughfares, and their contents were splashed on pedestrians by horses' hooves and the iron-tired wheels of wagons rumbling over cobblestones. Butchers threw animal guts in the street, where they attracted swarms of flies. Sometimes people tossed the contents of slop pots from windows. The better residential areas were clean and spacious, but people who had to get around town a great deal could hardly avoid neighborhoods where filth was casually accepted.

Granted that Burke had good reasons for buying a place in the country, he could still have enjoyed country air and the satisfaction of owning his own home on a plot of ground much smaller than 600 acres. Why didn't he buy something on a more modest scale?

The reason seems to have been that he actually thought of himself as wealthy in 1768. He had always shared a common purse with his brother Richard and with Will Burke, and they had just made an enormous fortune from speculations in East India Company stock. They would live at Beaconsfield and share expenses with him. Dr. Nugent couldn't do so because he had to keep up his practice in London, but he would be a frequent visitor. The trouble with the Burke "fortune" was that it existed only on paper. Nobody had the ready cash to make the down payment on Beaconsfield. That didn't matter. Will had a wealthy friend, Lord Verney. Lord Verney, who may have been as soft in the head as he was in the heart, cheerfully lent Will 6,000 pounds, to be repaid when Will's ship came in.

But even before the Burkes had settled in Beaconsfield, their troubles began. On June 12, 1768, the former owner of the estate died. The trustees named in his will sued Burke, demanding immediate payment of mortgages he had expected to pay off over many years. In desperation, he turned to his wealthy friends for help.

The next blow was a stock market crash in 1769. The "enormous fortune" evaporated. Lord Verney had taken Will Burke's advice on investments and had suffered such heavy losses that he couldn't — or wouldn't — lend any more money. Who can blame him? Again Burke had to beg his wealthy friends for loans far beyond his ability to repay. One thing should be said of him, and that is that those friends thought so much of him they would "lend" him huge sums, knowing they could not expect repayment.

So he managed to hold onto Beaconsfield. It brought him some income, since he made himself an expert on farming and sold farm produce. He also got rents from tenants on his property. Besides, Beaconsfield had a value that couldn't be measured in money. As a Member of Parliament Burke needed a place to entertain colleagues and offer hospitality to distinguished foreign visitors. Most important of all, living at Beaconsfield would give ten-year-old Richard Burke advantages. He would meet notable men at his father's table. He would be greeted with special respect by servants and tenants and thus acquire high self-esteem. He would not, like his father, suffer from a feeling of inferiority in the presence of those who had always been accustomed to a high style of living.

Burke's estate in the parish of Beaconsfield was called both Butler's Court and Gregories, but Burke preferred to date his letters from Beaconsfield, a little post town a mile away from his house. The two-storied house had large wings on either side of the central square, and its halls were colonnaded with Corinthian columns. From a distance it looked like a royal residence. It stood on a gentle slope and commanded a panoramic view of the surrounding countryside. It was only six miles north of Windsor Castle and Eton. Before and after Burke's lifetime that area has had great literary and historical associations. Burke's estate formed part of a manor that once belonged to Edmund Waller, a seventeenth-century poet. Other famous persons who have lived in or near Beaconsfield include John Milton, William Penn, and Benjamin Disraeli.

Even though Burke never actually "owned" Beaconsfield, he did get pleasure out of acting as its owner. He loved to invite people there either for a meal or for a prolonged stay. Many visitors left records of Beaconsfield in letters and diaries, and nearly everyone described it in glowing terms. Meals were always bountiful, and most of the food was raised on the grounds. At a typical meal the guests reported that they were served boiled turkey, roast beef, calf's head, woodcock — and that's not even mentioning an array of vegetables, custards, jellies, beverages.

Fine food was not reserved for distinguished guests. One day, when the Burkes were expecting some distinguished visitors, the housekeeper prepared a special dish for them. But when the visitors failed to show up, she kept back that dish, considering it too fine for George Crabbe, an impoverished poet whom Burke had rescued from a debtors' prison. Crabbe was at that time the only guest staying at Beaconsfield. Jane Burke, hearing the housekeeper's explanation for not putting the dish on the table, said, "What! Is not Mr. Crabbe here? Let it be brought up immediately."

The most memorable report about Beaconsfield is the one written by the dipped-in-acid pen of Mrs. Hester Thrale. She was the wife of a wealthy brewer, a vivacious little woman who cultivated friendships with literary people and set herself up to judge them with the kind of malice that is not uncommon in those who possess less talent than the objects of their judgment. At one time she compiled report cards of her literary friends, grading them on a scale of 0 to 20. These are the grades that she gave to Burke: Wit — 0; Humor — 0; Good Nature — 0; Religion — 0; Morality — 10; Scholarship — 14; Person and Voice — 10; General Knowledge — 19. Fortunately for Burke, hers was not the final judgment of his merits. Yet her opinion of his lack of humor may have been sadly close to the truth. Even Samuel Johnson, who esteemed Burke and would certainly have given him higher grades than those assigned by Mrs. Thrale, once said, "I never knew Burke to make a good joke in my life." It's too bad. We might like Burke better if he had had a less serious cast of mind. Yet it would be wrong to assume he always went around with a long face. He did have his lighter moments. Despite his spells of depression, he was usually able to conceal his low spirits from all but those who knew him intimately.

Burke's wit, or lack thereof, became the subject of some mildly amusing correspondence in 1786, when his friend James Boswell wrote to him, apologizing for having quoted Johnson's remark about Burke's lack of humor in a book entitled *Journal of a Tour of the Hebrides*. Boswell wanted to assure Burke that he had added a footnote to the quotation from Johnson. In the footnote Boswell quoted several specimens of Burke's wit. Burke was actually fond of puns that had the grace of an arthritic elephant.

Burke, in reply to Boswell's letter, thanked him for his solicitude, adding: "The Reputation for Wit (the *fama dicacis*) is what I certainly am not entitled to; and, I think, I never aimed at. If I had been so ambitious, I must shew myself as deficient in Judgment as I am in wit, if I thought that a Title to pleasantry could be made out by argument."

Burke's letter goes on to elaborate on these points at tedious length. Let it suffice to say that a book entitled *The Wit and Humor of Edmund Burke* would be a thin volume.

To a friend as close as Richard Shackleton he could be frank in admitting his mood swings. And once, in a letter to the Marquess of Rockingham (September, 1774) he wrote:

Sometimes when I am alone, in spite of all my efforts I fall into a melancholy which is inexpressible, and to which, if I gave way, I should not continue long under it, but must totally sink. Yet I do assure you that partly and principally by the force of natural good spirits, and partly by a strong sense of what I ought to do, I bear up well, that no one who did not know them could easily discover the state of my mind or my circumstances.

Following a visit to Beaconsfield, Mrs. Thrale published

an account in which she described it as "delightful." But the notes she made in her diary told a different story. There she mentioned Burke's heavy drinking and the "Dirt, Cobwebs, Pictures and Statues that would not have disgraced the City of Paris itself, where Misery and Magnificence reign in all their splendour and in perfect Amity. (Note, Irish Roman Catholics are always like the foreigners somehow, dirty and dressy with all their clothes hanging as if upon a Peg.) That Mrs. Burke drinks as well as her husband and that their black-a-moor carries Tea around with a cut finger wrapped in Rags must help to apologize for the severity with which I have treated so very distinguished a Character."

Her description may have been accurate, yet it conveyed a misleading impression. Burke did drink heavily at times. In his letters he described occasions when he and other guests at a celebration drank themselves under the table. Yet he probably drank less than most men of his day. Among the nobility heavy drinking — especially of port wine — was so common that the expression "drunk as a lord" came into the language during the eighteenth century.

Whether Jane was excessively fond of the bottle we do not know. It may be that she enjoyed only a glass or two during Mrs. Thrale's visit. And Mrs. Thrale is the only person who spoke unfavorably of Jane. Everyone else seemed to regard Jane as almost too good to be true. It is almost a relief to learn that, in addition to her other virtues, she did not make a hobby of digging dirt out of corners. Mrs. Thrale, who had a large staff of servants, had no sympathy with Jane, who couldn't possibly afford enough servants to keep Beaconsfield in perfect order. The Burkes themselves did much of the work in their house and on the grounds. They would drive up to their front door in a coach driven by four black horses, but next day those same horses would be used to pull a plow. And visitors, seeing Burke laboring in the fields, sometimes took him for a farmhand.

That coach must often have been in use to transport not only the Burke family but many of their guests. When Burke's old teacher, Abraham Shackleton, visited Beaconsfield in the summer of 1769, he considered the elegance of that coach so overpowering that he was reluctant to ride in such style. Shackleton's granddaughter Mary says in her memoirs:

> His illustrious pupil Edmund Burke prevailed on him to pay him a visit at Beaconsfield, and sent his coach to convey him thither. My grandfather shrank from the idea of riding in such a grand coach, and offered Burke's servant half-a-guinea to permit him to travel on his own horse, but the servant firmly refused; and, however reluctant, the humble man had to consent to be conveyed in unwelcome pomp.

Mrs. Thrale's comments about the paintings and sculptures at Beaconsfield indicate that she was more impressed with their nudity than with their artistic merits. Some may have been in questionable taste. Burke did not select them. He had to take them as part of the property when he bought the estate. But Joshua Reynolds (who was knighted in 1769 and thereafter referred to as "Sir") said that the collection included some fine pieces by sixteenth- and seventeenth-century French and Italian artists. At any rate, the collection was so large that it sprawled all over the mansion — in the halls, the library, the dining room, the drawing room, even the housekeeper's apartment. But Burke was not the kind of collector who appreciates artists only after they are dead. He added to the original collection by buying paintings of living artists, including several portraits by Joshua Reynolds. He also helped young artists by paying for their education, introducing them to people who could help them, and sometimes completely supporting them during their years of struggle. One form of waste he could not tolerate was the waste of human talent.

Nobody who visited Beaconsfield ever left a report of the library, and Burke himself seems never to have referred to it in his letters. Not until the estate was sold in 1833 was a catalogue of its contents compiled. Over the years Burke had evidently added many books to the original collection — books that he had bought, books received as gifts, perhaps some review copies from the days when he was editor of the *Annual Register*. The collection indicated a remarkable catholicity of taste. It indicated, too, that he was a reader and not simply a collector. By the time of his death that library included books on economics, history, law and the constitution, public affairs, travel, classical antiquity, belles lettres, science and medicine, religion and philosophy, drama and art. The collections of books about Ireland, India, and America were particularly large.

8. Meanwhile, Back in America
(1765-1773)

BURKE'S PATRON, THE Marquess of Rockingham, held the post of Prime Minister for only one year and twenty days. During the early months of his administration he worked hard, but he lacked the drive to go on working at such a brisk pace. Horse racing meant more to him than politics. By the fall of 1768 he was spending most of his time at the race track. Burke became frantic when he saw that not only Rockingham but most of Rockingham's supporters were failing to show up in Parliament. Burke took upon himself the function of serving as their "whip" — a term he originated to describe the person who rounds up legislators when their votes are needed.

Brief though the Rockingham administration was, it lasted long enough for Burke to establish an enduring friendship with Rockingham. In spite of their different backgrounds, each could appreciate the virtues of the other. Rockingham was, in Burke's eyes, an example of the kind of aristocrat who had much to give to his country because he was fundamentally an honest man, a decent man, a man whose special advantages qualified him to handle sticky situations with skill and grace. True, he was inclined to be indolent, but one could not expect tremendous drive in a man who had never to struggle for the advantages he enjoyed. Burke was the one with the drive, and Rockingham admired that drive, as he admired most of the things he knew about Burke. The Burkes and the Rockinghams saw each other socially quite often, and there was no hint of condescension on the part of the Rockinghams, no hint of servility on the part of the Burkes. There was simply mutual respect.

Burke strongly believed in an aristocratic class. He felt that the best government is that which is conducted by those who, by reason of property and long connection with the nation's history, have a patriotic interest rooted in the nation's soil. In a letter to the Duke of Richmond, Burke wrote:

> Persons in your station of life ought to have long views. You people of great families and hereditary trusts and fortunes, are not like such as I am, who, whatever we may be, by the rapidity of our growth, and even by the fruit we bear, and flatter ourselves that, while we creep on the ground, or belly into melons, that are exquisite for size and flavour, yet still are but annual plants, that perish with our season, and leave no sort of traces behind us. You, if you are what you ought to be, are in my eye the great oaks that shade a country, and perpetuate your benefits from generation to generation.

This is a rather fancy way of saying "noblesse oblige" — or that those who hold high rank have a moral obligation to use their advantages for the benefit of their country. But Burke was not overawed by mere titles. He had only contempt for aristocrats who took selfish advantage of their privileges. Those aristocrats with whom he became friendly were a select group of men who had given good service in Parliament. But even those men did not always take their duties seriously enough to suit Burke. He had to keep prodding them to show up in Parliament when they would have preferred to enjoy the comforts of their country estates.

After King George dismissed Rockingham as Prime Minister, Burke wrote a pamphlet in which he summed up the achievements of Rockingham's administration. That administration, Burke said, had seen the Americans becalmed, Englishmen confirmed in their liberties, trade and manufacture expanded, and the king's business handled efficiently. The purpose of the pamphlet, of course, was to suggest that England would not again enjoy such efficient government until Rockingham was reappointed. But the king had had enough of Rockingham. He chose William Pitt as the new Prime Minister. But Pitt was now in such poor health that he was able to hold that post only briefly. The Duke of Grafton became nominally Prime Minister.

The Duke of Grafton had no skill as a political leader. He couldn't function at all without the help of someone as experienced as William Pitt. To flatter Pitt and thus make him willing to serve as a consultant, the king offered him the title of Earl of Chatham. Pitt snapped at the honor — much to the disgust of his former admirers, who had affectionately called him "the Great Commoner." His popularity fell off sharply.

Shortly after he accepted the earldom, he succumbed to a spell of melancholia so severe that he couldn't — or wouldn't — speak a word. He locked himself up in a room and had his meals passed through a hatch in the door. When he wanted something, he would thump on the floor with a cane and signify what he wanted with gestures. For hours on end he would sit at a table, resting his head on his hands. The voice that had thundered on behalf of the Americans was silenced. Would it ever be heard again?

Without Pitt's help Grafton could do nothing. So he didn't even try. Now he spent most of his time with his mistress. Somebody had to take over the reins of government, and that somebody turned out to be Charles Townshend, Chancellor of the Exchequeur. Townshend was charming, witty, frivolous. He was nicknamed "Champagne Charley" because of his fondness for the beverage and his ability to speak brilliantly while under its influence. Now he functioned as Prime Minister without actually holding the title, and the delicious taste of power made him reckless.

By the beginning of 1767 the colonists were in trouble again. This time they were rebelling against the Quartering Act, which required them to provide food and lodging for British troops stationed in America. One objectionable feature of this act was that it hit some colonies much harder than it hit others. New York, as a port of disembarkation and a military center, would have to support many more troops than other colonies. Therefore, the New York Assembly flatly refused to comply with the act. Now Parliament had to decide how to punish New York.

During the debate former Prime Minister Grenville, who had been responsible for the Quartering Act, became enraged when Townshend ridiculed him. Grenville shouted, "You are cowards! You are afraid of the Americans! You dare not tax America!"

"Dare not tax America?" Townshend shot back. "I dare tax America!"

"Dare you tax America!" Grenville exploded. "I wish to God I could see it!"

"I will! I will!" As usual, Townshend was tipsy. Now, to prove that he knew how to squeeze money out of the Americans, he proposed new taxes on glass, lead, paints, paper, and tea. And he was eloquent enough to persuade Parliament to vote for those taxes. On June 29, 1767, the Townshend Acts became law. Burke was one of the few who opposed them.

Shortly after news of the Townshend Acts reached America, Townshend died suddenly at the age of forty-five. He would never know what a storm he had brewed by his impulsive behavior.

The American reaction to the Townshend Acts was less violent than their reaction to the Stamp Act. But there was considerable violence. It wasn't the duties as such that the Americans found objectionable. Townshend had cleverly proposed "external" rather than "internal" taxes because

Americans claimed, at the time of the Stamp Act, that what they objected to was "internal" taxes. Far more dangerous than the duties were other features of the acts. They required taxes to be paid in coins rather than paper, and the supply of coins in the colonies was distressingly low. They called for reorganization of the customs service, with courts of admiralty established in the colonies to expedite cases of smuggling. They reaffirmed the writs of assistance, which gave treasury officials the right to search a man's home, warehouse, or ship without a search warrant. One of the acts dissolved the New York Assembly until it had met the cost of quartering British troops. Any surplus from the revenue was to be used to pay British colonial officials and thus make them independent of colonial assemblies. The colonists' chief weapon against truculent governors had been the power to withhold their salaries. Now the colonists were robbed of that weapon. They had no way of controlling their governors.

The Stamp Act crisis had taught the Americans that they could hurt England by refusing to buy goods manufactured in England. Now they used that weapon with even greater effect. They did such a good job of crippling English industries that most of the Townshend Acts were repealed in the spring of 1770. But Parliament had to prove that it did have the right to tax the colonies. As token of that right, Parliament kept the tax on tea. For a time it seemed as if this idea would work.

After the American colonies calmed down, Burke was under less pressure than during the crisis situations. In February, 1773, he found time to visit France, where he took his son Richard to place him in the care of a bishop for a year. Richard, now fifteen, had been at the top of his class at the Westminster School. A year in France would put a polish on his preparatory education and enable him to acquire a fluent command of French. Burke himself could speak French haltingly. He wanted Richard to do better than that. After Richard returned to England, he would enter Oxford University, and his year on the Continent would be a great asset to him.

While Burke was in France, he was presented to King Louis XV at Versailles. There he saw the seventeen-year-old Dauphiness Marie Antoinette, whose beauty he described thus: "Surely never lighted on this orb, which she hardly seemed to touch, a more delightful vision. I saw her just above the horizon, decorating and cheering the elevated sphere she just began to move in — glittering like the morning star full of life and splendour and joy."

When he returned to England, he was full of stories about France to tell the members of the Club, which was at that time undergoing some changes. It had originally consisted of only nine members, since it was felt that a larger number would prevent free play of conversation. But its members were busy men, too busy to attend meetings regularly. Over the years a few more members had been added. Now it seemed like a good idea to increase the membership.

But before the new members were admitted, little Noll Goldsmith must enjoy his hour of glory. By this time he had won some distinction as a poet, novelist, and playwright. One of his plays, *She Stoops to Conquer*, had its premiere on March 15, 1773. The Club celebrated by dining at the Shakespeare Tavern before going on to the theater. Poor Goldsmith was so jittery that he could hardly swallow a bite. He had just learned of the death of the King of Sardinia and was afraid that this news might have a depressing effect on the audience. Burke dryly assured him that theatergoers were unlikely to be melancholy over the death of a potentate they had never heard of. But Goldsmith couldn't calm down. He didn't attend the theater with the others. If the audience should fail to laugh at what he considered his funniest lines, he'd writhe in agony. Let the others go to the theater. He would meanwhile pace up and down in a nearby park until told how the play was going.

By prearrangement the Club members sat in scattered places in the theater so that their applause would have a contagious effect. Samuel Johnson occupied a box, where he was visible to the entire audience. If he laughed at a scene, the audience would take it as a signal to roar. He did laugh. The play turned out to be Goldsmith's greatest success.

One of the new members admitted to the Club in the spring of 1773 was David Garrick. To celebrate his election, Mrs. Thrale — the woman who wrote catty comments about Beaconsfield — gave a party for the Club in her husband's brewery, with a table set on a huge brewing copper and beefsteaks cooked in the brewery furnace.

At about the same time the Club accepted another member, a Scotsman named James Boswell. Since he had several unappealing traits (he was a habitual sot, vain, inquisitive, garrulous, boring), most of the Club members had reservations about him. But he was sponsored by Samuel Johnson. That meant that no member dared blackball Boswell lest Johnson should blackball anyone whom any other member might sponsor. And a unanimous vote was required for admission. Thus, with the genuine support of only one dominant member, Boswell achieved a long-sought goal.

He did not, like Burke, achieve instant friendship with Johnson. Poor Boswell — or "Bozzy," as the Club members called him — had to plug away for ten years before Johnson saw fit to admit him to his intimate circle of friends. Boswell was so eager to meet Johnson that he hung around a bookseller's shop where Johnson was sure to show up. But when, on the evening of May 16, 1763, the outline of Johnson's massive figure showed through the glazed door, Boswell gasped in apprehension.

Rumors that Johnson hated everything related to Scotland actually had little foundation, but Boswell had heard such rumors. Now he begged Tom Davies, the bookseller, "Don't tell him where I come from."

It was poor psychology. When Davies made the introduction, he couldn't resist saying, "Mr. Boswell — from Scotland."

"I do indeed come from Scotland," Boswell stammered. "But I can't help it."

"That, Sir," thundered Johnson, "I find is what a very great number of your countrymen cannot help."

Still, having acknowledged the introduction in a way that might have pulverized anyone less persistent than Boswell, Johnson became more civil. He chatted pleasantly for a few minutes. After he left, Davies assured Boswell, "Don't be uneasy. I can see that he likes you well."

After this meeting Boswell seized every opportunity to tag at Johnson's heels and to ply him with questions. Sometimes those questions were rather inane. Once, for example, he asked Johnson, "If, Sir, you were shut up in a castle, and a newborn child with you, what would you do?"

Johnson replied, "Why, Sir, I should not much like my company."

Boswell persisted, "But would you take the trouble of rearing it?"

To this Johnson answered, "Why yes, Sir, I would, but I must have all conveniences."

What Boswell was actually trying to do in asking such a question was to find out what Johnson found so attractive in the Thrale family, with whom Johnson was living at the time. Mrs. Thrale had several small children, whose company Johnson enjoyed. And Boswell was jealous of Mrs. Thrale's close friendship with Johnson.

When Boswell was finally admitted to the Club, he turned out to be a very agreeable member. And it is good that he got to know the members well. Had he not attended meetings and kept records of the conversations, the world of literature would have lost a treasure.

He didn't record every word spoken at the Club meetings, of course. A full report of even a single session might well have run to dozens of pages. But his reports of some sessions were sufficiently complete to give a good idea of the cut and thrust of the conversation. The notes he made of one session, held on April 3, 1778, probably cover everything that was discussed that evening.

The conversation began with mention of a marble statue of a dog, valued at a thousand guineas. Johnson took the lead in suggesting reasons why a statue of an animal might be worth that much. Then Burke introduced the subject of emigration, and for several minutes the company talked about the relationship between overpopulation and destructive diseases.

Dramatist Richard Brinsley Sheridan then said to Burke: "Mr. Burke, I don't mean to flatter, but when posterity reads one of your speeches in Parliament, it will be difficult to believe that you took so much pains, knowing with certainty that it would produce no effect, that not one vote would be gained by it."

Burke replied that he considered it very well worth while for a man to take pains to speak well in Parliament. "If a man speaks well, he gradually establishes a certain reputation and consequence in general opinion, which sooner or later will have its political reward. Besides, though not one vote is gained, a good speech has its effect. Though an act which has been ably opposed passes into a law, yet in its progress it is modelled, it is softened in such a manner that we see plainly the Minister has been told, that the members attached to him are so sensible of its injustice or absurdity from what they have heard, that it must be altered."

Burke then talked about the Irish language, a topic that led to mention of travel books and a discussion of why authors of such books usually seem to be displeased with the countries they visit. This led to the subject of human nature.

Burke observed: "From the experience which I have had — and I have had a great deal — I have learned to think *better* of mankind."

Johnson said: "From my experience I have found them worse in commercial dealings, more disposed to cheat, than I had any notion of; but more disposed to do one another good than I had conceived. And really it is wonderful, considering how much attention is necessary for men to take care of themselves and ward off immediate evils which press upon them, it is wonderful how much they do for others. And it is said of the greatest liar, that he tells more truth than falsehood; so it may be said of the worst man, that he does more good than evil."

Boswell now tried to cut in with: "Perhaps from experience men may be found *happier* than we suppose."

But Johnson rejoined: "No, sir. The more we inquire, we shall find men the less happy."

They went on to discuss virtue and temptation. Johnson raised the question of how far a man has the right to subject another man to temptations that may prove too strong for him.

The meeting closed with the passing of a resolution that Johnson should write a letter, on behalf of the Club, to a gentleman who had offered to send them a hogshead of claret once their present supply ran low.

Drawing on records of meetings of the Club, as well as records of his many other encounters with Johnson, Boswell would one day write a biography of Johnson that is considered a classic. Boswell's notebooks sparkle with details of Johnson's behavior, details so vivid that Johnson still lives on the printed page long after many of his written words have become of little interest to anyone but literary scholars.

Mrs. Hester Thrale also wrote a biography of Samuel Johnson. She prided herself on having literary talent (not without some justification), and she did know Johnson very well. After she met him in 1765, she proceeded to make a pet of him, inviting him to live in an apartment at her home. Since she knew that his wig was always singed because of his habit of reading with his head close to the candle, she kept a supply of wigs on hand and had her valet give him a fresh wig whenever he was called to the dinner table. She also allowed him to compile her library and to use that library for his own research. Johnson, a heartbroken widower since the death of his wife in 1752, found Mrs. Thrale fascinating. Her youth (she was thirty-one years his junior) and her vivacious personality were like a tonic to him and helped him to cope with his spells of depression. Mrs. Thrale had as much right as Boswell to feel that she was qualified to write a biography of Johnson. But her biography can't compare with Boswell's. Few biographies can.

For a time after Boswell's admission to the Club, Burke treated him with urbane condescension. But Boswell, for all that he could be annoying, was hard to dislike. Burke did come to like him as he got to know him better. And Burke was probably not above being flattered at indications that Boswell greatly admired him. Boswell expressed that admiration in the notes he took on April 3, 1773, when for the first time he heard Burke speak in the House of Commons:

> It was astonishing how all kinds of figures of speech crowded upon him. He was like a man in an Orchard where boughs loaded with fruit hung around him, and he pulled apples as fast as he pleased and pelted the ministry. It seemed to me however that this Oratory rather tended to distinguish himself than to assist his cause. There was amusement instead of persuasion. It was like the exhibition of a favourite Actor. But I would have been exceedingly happy to be him.

Impressed though Boswell was with Burke's eloquence, he put his finger on one of Burke's weaknesses — a tendency to deliver dazzlingly brilliant speeches for the sheer delight of demonstrating his oratorical skill.

Boswell's opinion of Burke's oratorical style was shared by other shrewd observers. Horace Walpole echoes Boswell's sentiments in a comment recorded in his *Memoirs:*

> He was so fond of flowers, that he snatched them, if they presented themselves, even from Ovid's *Metamorphoses . . .*

Aiming always at the brilliant, and rarely concise, it appeared that he felt nothing really but the lust of applause. His knowledge was infinite, but vanity had the only key to it, and though no doubt he aspired highly, he seemed content when he had satisfied the glory of the day, whatever proved the event of the debate. This kind of eloquence contented himself, and often his party; but the House grew weary at length of so many essays. Having come too late into public life, and being too conceited to study men whom he thought his inferiors in ability, he proved a very indifferent politician — the case of many men I have known who have dealt too much in books or a profession.

Not long after Burke made the speech mentioned by Boswell, the House of Commons passed a resolution that would create more trouble in the colonies.

The Americans were not overconcerned when Parliament decided to retain the tax on tea. They simply resorted to their old weapon of nonimportation and refused to buy tea from the British East India Company. The result was that the company was now on the brink of bankruptcy. It had seventeen million pounds of tea stored in English warehouses, and few orders were coming in from abroad. Americans were getting all the tea they wanted by smuggling it from the Dutch and French West Indies. And that wasn't funny — to the English. Since the British East India Company ran the prosperous Indian empire, England was now in grave danger of losing that empire.

Parliament decided that what the Americans really wanted was tea at a bargain price. To encourage the Americans to buy tea from England instead of from smugglers, the price was reduced so that, even with an excise tax of threepence a pound, it was now lower than the price of smuggled tea. A neat way of handling the problem, in the opinion of those who voted for the new legislation.

Forthwith clippers laden with tea set sail for Boston, New York, Philadelphia, and Charleston.

9. Vengeance for a Tea Party
(1774)

BEFORE THE TEA CLIPPERS reached America, faster ships had brought news of the new act to the colonies. Riots broke out in the port cities. In New York and Philadelphia enraged citizens refused to let the tea clippers land their cargo. In Charleston customs authorities seized the tea and refused to pay duty on it.

But in Boston Governor Thomas Hutchinson refused to be intimidated by the mob. He would not give clearance papers until the duty on the tea had been paid. On the afternoon of December 16 seven thousand Bostonians gathered at the Old South Church to hear the latest word from Hutchinson. There wasn't room for everyone inside the church, of course. Thousands stood outside in the chilly rain. When it was announced that Hutchinson still refused clearance papers, the crowd let out a war whoop. Several hundred men, some disguised as Indians, surged toward Griffin's Wharf. There they boarded the three tea clippers and dumped 342 chests of tea into Boston harbor.

What would King George say, what would he do, when he heard about it? The people of Boston would not find out for several months. During those months Edmund Burke would be shouting himself hoarse to defend Boston from the wrath of King George and Parliament.

But on April 4, 1774, while Parliament was debating how to punish Boston, Burke heard news that made him break down in sobs. NOLL GOLDSMITH WAS DEAD!

The news came as a shock. Nobody had realized that Goldsmith was seriously ill. He was only forty-four. And he had just begun to enjoy the sweet taste of success that meant so much to him. Burke had known him longer than anyone in London. Now memories of Goldsmith flooded back: the young sizar perpetually lounging at the gates of Trinity College, an older Goldsmith filling page after page with hack writing assignments, a smiling Goldsmith all aflutter over the success of *She Stoops to Conquer*. Now no more words would flow from the Goldsmith pen.

Even more than Burke, Sir Joshua Reynolds was shattered at the news. He dropped his brush and would not paint another stroke that day. This was more remarkable than it may seem, for he had extraordinarily methodical working habits. Even a bereavement in his immediate family never prevented him from doing his daily stint of painting. He painted even on Sundays, much to the dismay of Samuel Johnson, who would have considered himself doomed to eternal perdition if he ever violated the Sabbath.

Goldsmith had been Sir Joshua's closest friend. A portrait of Goldsmith by Reynolds showed a tender appreciation of the poet's essential nature. Instead of portraying him in the tasteless finery and wig he wore in public, Reynolds showed him as he looked while working at home, wearing a simple shirt open at the throat. The painting did not lie about Goldsmith's features. Yet it brought out his lovable qualities. Goldsmith, in turn, was fond of Reynolds. He dedicated his poem *The Deserted Village* to him in these words: "The only dedication I ever made was to my brother, because I loved him better than most other men. He is since dead. Permit me to inscribe this poem to you."

But Goldsmith was mourned by many besides his brilliant, famous friends. When the news spread that the little

Irishman had died at dawn on that April day, the staircase of his home at Brick Court was filled with weeping men and women, most of them of the poorest class. Many were unfamiliar with his writings. They mourned him for his endearing personality.

Burke and Reynolds, together with other friends of Goldsmith, started to make plans for a public funeral. But they decided against elaborate display after they learned about Goldsmith's financial circumstances. He owed more than two thousand pounds when he died, and his friends chipped in to pay off the debt. When Johnson heard the size of the debt, he exclaimed, "Was ever poet so trusted before?" The idea was rather pleasing to Johnson. To *owe* two thousand pounds was the next best thing to *owning* it.

When a monument to Goldsmith, executed by Joseph Nollekens, was erected at Westminster Abbey, Johnson composed a Latin inscription. Several of the Club members, including Burke, sent a tactful note to Johnson, praising the inscription he had composed, but suggesting it would be better to have the inscription written in English, "as we think that the Memory of so Eminent an English Writer ought to be perpetuated in the language to which his Works are likely to be so lasting an Ornament." Johnson insisted that he would never disgrace the walls of Westminster Abbey with an English inscription. The Latin text remains. Its most famous phrase reads: *Nullum quod tetigit non ornavit* (He touched nothing that he did not adorn).

After Goldsmith's funeral, Burke returned to the House of Commons to continue his fight on behalf of the Americans. On the evening of April 19, 1774, he delivered a two-hour speech on American taxation.

The duty on tea, he said, should be repealed for the sake of tolerable relations with America, for the sake of the British East India Company, for the sake of the imperial system.

Be content to bind America by laws of trade, you have always done it. Let this be your reason for binding their trade. Do not burden them by taxes; you were not used to do so from the beginning. Let this be your reason for not taxing. But if, intemperately, unwisely, fatally, you sophisticate and poison the very source of government, by urging subtle deductions, and consequences odious to those you govern, from the unlimited and illimitable nature of supreme sovereignty, you will teach them by these means to call that sovereignty itself in question. When you drive him hard, the boar will surely turn upon the hunters. If that sovereignty and their freedom cannot be reconciled, which will they take? They will cast your sovereignty in your face. Nobody will be argued into slavery.

Had these words been heeded, the course of American history would have been very different. America would eventually have broken away from England. A rapidly growing nation with great natural resources would not have indefinitely remained tied to the apron strings of the mother country. But the break might have been accomplished without bloodshed many years later. Unfortunately, in this situation as in many others, Burke was more farsighted than his colleagues. Parliament was never in so vindictive a mood as when it learned what Boston had done with the precious cargo of tea. Now Boston must be punished in a way that would teach all Americans a good lesson. Votes in favor of the Coercive Acts were so heavy that no roll call was needed.

British warships sealed off Boston harbor on June 1, the date on which the first of these acts, the Boston Port Act, went into effect. All water traffic ceased. All business in Boston came to a standstill. The people of Boston had no way to make a living. Yet they were expected to pay for the tea that they had destroyed — eighteen thousand pounds' worth — plus the cost of supporting British troops stationed in Boston. Bostonians were so stunned by the punishment that they held a mass meeting at Faneuil Hall and got down on their knees to pray.

Lord North, who had been Prime Minister since 1770, assumed that the other American port cities would be overjoyed at Boston's misfortune. They would benefit by getting the trade Boston had lost.

How little he understood Americans!

When news of the Boston Port Act reached Boston on May 10, couriers had galloped southward to spread the news. By June 1 all of the colonies knew about it. On that day, throughout the colonies, preachers delivered fiery sermons. Shops closed their shutters. Flags hung at half-staff. Muffled church bells tolled at intervals throughout the day.

The colonies did more than offer token support to Boston. Getting foodstuffs and supplies to the troubled city was difficult. Now that Boston harbor was closed off, the only access to the city was over a narrow neck of land that connected it with the mainland. Wagon after wagon rolled over the narrow neck of land, bringing gifts to Boston from other Massachusetts towns and from all the other colonies.

On June 2 a ship arrived in Boston with news of the other Coercive Acts. All disturbers of the king's peace were to be transported to England for trial. All judges and officers of the courts were to be appointed by the king. No town meetings could be held without the written consent of the governor. British troops were authorized to quarter their troops in the homes of private citizens.

Then the king's regiments arrived. White tents and frowning cannon covered Boston Common. Everywhere Bostonians turned, they saw the glitter of bayonets and the flash of redcoats. Salt was constantly being poured into their wounds.

On June 17 the Massachusetts Assembly invited the other colonies to send delegates to a congress to be held in Philadelphia in September. The purpose of the congress — which would be known as the First Continental Congress — was to discuss the Coercive Acts. (The colonists called them "the Intolerable Acts.") At the congress, which opened on September 5, almost every shade of opinion in the colonies was represented by the fifty-six delegates, but the more militant delegates ran the show. On the final day of the congress, October 26, the delegates drafted a petition to King George.

But news of the congress took several weeks to cross the Atlantic. Before King George knew anything about it, he had called for new elections.

Burke had been a Member of Parliament for nearly nine years. At forty-five he was the veteran of many debates and had acquired a statesmanlike air. Now he wore steel-framed, square-lensed spectacles that had a way of slipping halfway down his prominent nose. Those spectacles had been added to caricatures of him, with the nose greatly exaggerated in size, as if to suggest that he was always sticking it into things that were none of his business.

But if his growing reputation had made him the target of such abuse, it had also won him much respect. He was so well known as a champion of British commercial interests that the merchants of Bristol invited him to become a candidate to represent their city in Parliament. Bristol, second largest port in England, located on the west coast, had suffered keenly from the loss of American trade. Many Bristol residents had close relatives in America and sympathized with the Americans for that reason, too. Moreover, Bristol had an exceptionally large number of qualified voters — approximately 5,000 out of a total population of 75,000. And that number could be increased by bringing in voters from other parts of England, since there were no residence requirements for voters. Any candidate who could afford the expense of transporting voters could greatly improve his chances of being elected.

Burke, of course, couldn't afford to pay campaign expenses out of his own pocket. But he had the support of wealthy citizens of Bristol. On November 3, 1774, after an arduous campaign, he was elected. He delivered an address of thanks to his supporters, in which he promised to heed their opinions and to prefer their interests to his own. But he made a distinction between opinions and judgment. Parliament was a deliberative assembly, he said, not a congress of ambassadors. If his constituents' instructions should conflict with his judgment, he would have to put the general good before local interests. "Your faithful, your devoted servant I shall be to the end of my life, a flatterer you do not wish for." In later years Burke would boast that he was "the first man who on the hustings, at a popular election, rejected the authority of instructions from constituents."

Burke's campaign in Bristol led to a lasting friendship with one of his supporters, a Quaker named Richard Champion. In future years the Champions and the Burkes wrote to each other frequently and often visited each other.

By this time Burke had for some years been a friend of Benjamin Franklin, agent for the colonies of Massachusetts, New Jersey, and Pennslyvania. Burke, too, was an agent for an American colony — New York. He was selected for the post in 1770, at a salary of five hundred pounds a year. It may seem odd that a member of Parliament should hold such a position, but that sort of thing was customary at the time. He continued to serve as agent for New York until 1775.

On December 12, 1774, Benjamin Franklin sent Burke the following note:

Having just received a Petition from the American Congress to the King, with a letter directed to the North American Agents among whom you are named; this is to request you would be pleased to meet the other Agents tomorrow Noon, at Waghorn's Coffeehouse, Westminster, in order to consider the said letter, and agree upon the time and manner of presenting the Petition,

I am,
Sir,
Your most obedient
humble servant
B. Franklin

Burke did not accept the invitation, on the ground that he had not received instructions from the New York Assembly to do so. The *Public Advertiser,* on January 22, 1775, published this statement:

> We hear that a celebrated Orator and Patriot was waited on by the Gentlemen commissioned with the Petition of the Congress to the King, requesting him to present it to his Majesty; but that Gentleman positively refused it, by saying, "As he knew of no Legal Meeting called a congress, he could not, in Justification to his character, be their Representative."

Knowing how concerned Burke was with serious matters at the time, it is diverting to know about a conversation in lighter vein he had with Boswell on April 6, 1775:

> I maintained a strange proposition to Burke: that it was better for a Scotsman and an Irishman to preserve so much of their native accent as not to be quite perfect in English, because it was unnatural. I would have all the birds of the air to retain somewhat of their own notes: a blackbird to sing like a blackbird, and a thrush like a thrush, and not a blackbird and other birds to sing all like some other bird. Burke agreed with me. "Englishmen would laugh heartily, and say, 'Here an Irishman and a Scotsman, each with his own country tone strong, attempt to prove that it is better to have it.'"
> I said it was unnatural to hear a Scotsman speaking perfect English. He appeared a machine. I instanced Wedderburn. "A man of wood," said I, "or a man of brass."
> "Ay, a man of brass," cried Burke.
> Lord Lisburne and I had afterwards a dispute on this subject. My metaphor of the birds he opposed by saying, "A Scotsman may do very well with his own tone in Coll; but if he comes into the House of Commons, it will be better if he speaks English. A bagpipe may do very well in the Highlands, but I would not introduce it into Bach's concert."
> "This," said I, "shows what it is to argue in metaphors. One is just as good as another. But I maintained to my Lord that it put me in a passion to hear a Scotsman speaking in a perfect English tone. It was a false voice. He speaks as if he had some

pipe or speaking instrument in his mouth. And I thought always, "Can't he take this confounded pipe out, and let us hear him speak with his own organs?" I do still think I am right. Lord Lisburne and Sir Gilbert Elliot had just a little of the Scotch accent. "Well," said I, "he has just what I wish as much of the native note as to mark his species." I said to Burke, "You would not have a man use Scotch words, as to say a *trance* for a *passage* in a house."

"No," said he, "that is a different language."

"But," said I, "is it not better, too, to try to pronounce not in the broad Scotch way and to say *passage* and not pawssage?"

"Yes," said Burke, "when once you're taught how they pronounce in England, but don't try at English pronunciation."

On the day following this conversation Johnson made his oft-quoted comment, "Patriotism is the last refuge of scoundrels."

Reynolds and Boswell insisted that all patriots were not scoundrels, mentioning Burke as an example of one who was not.

Johnson retorted: "I do not say that Burke is not honest. But we have no reason to conclude from his political conduct that he is so. Were Burke to accept of a place from this ministry, he would lose that character for firmness which he has, and might be turned out of his place in a year. This ministry is neither stable nor grateful to their friends as Sir Robert Walpole was. So that Burke may think it more for his interest to take his chance of the Rockingham Party coming in."

10. A Great Speech and a Little Battle
(1775)

BURKE AND JOHNSON stood at opposite poles in their political views. To put it simply, Burke was a Whig and Johnson was a Tory. Actually, political views in the eighteenth century could not be characterized quite so simply. The words "Whig" and "Tory," introduced during the seventeenth century, originally had unfavorable meanings. "Whig" meant horse thief. "Tory" meant outlaw. In time the words lost their original connotations. Whig Members of Parliament included great landowners, aristocrats, city interests. Tories were usually rural squires. The Whigs had a tradition of keeping the monarchy in its place. The Tories had a tradition of supporting the monarchy.

To be a close friend of a politician and to avoid discussing politics with him is virtually impossible. But that is what Johnson managed to do. He loved to talk with Burke. He would have been heartbroken if anything disrupted their friendship. So they came to an understanding that they would avoid discussing politics. The arrangement worked because both of them knew so much about other things that they were never at a loss for subjects to discuss.

They needed the stimulation and comfort each got from the other. Both of them were subject to spells of melancholia, but with Johnson those spells were probably far more severe than with Burke. At times Johnson felt so depressed that he couldn't see anyone but his doctor, who once told Boswell of something that Johnson said during such a spell: "I would consent to have a limb amputated to recover my spirits." The loss of Burke's friendship might well have been more than Johnson could endure.

On matters less controversial than the American situation Burke and Johnson were likely to disagree if for no better reason than that disagreement makes for lively debates. But at one time, when Johnson was quite sick, he said, "That fellow calls forth all my powers. Were I to see Burke now, it would kill me."

During the early months of 1775 the situation in America became so grave that everyone was talking about it. It was impossible for an intelligent person to have no opinions on the subject. Johnson and Burke may well have tried to avoid each other at that time rather than run the risk of an argument that both would have cause to regret bitterly.

Johnson didn't know much about Americans. What he did know he didn't like. He was disgusted at the way they had behaved ever since the Stamp Act was passed, and he made no secret of his disgust. "Why is it," he asked, "that we hear the loudest yelps for liberty from the drivers of Negroes?" And he said that the Americans were "a race of convicts and ought to be thankful for anything we allow them short of hanging."

Johnson, with justification, is often cited as having a compassionate attitude toward the victims of slavery that was shared by few of his contemporaries. Boswell once observed how passionately Johnson defended an escaped slave who was trying to claim his liberty in a Scottish court. Boswell also once quoted Johnson as having proposed a toast while in the company of several Oxford scholars: "Here's to the next insurrection of the negroes in the West Indies."

In this connection, it should be noted that the principal beneficiary named in Johnson's will was Francis Barber, a

Jamaican-born black man who had been entrusted to Johnson's care as a young boy and who had for many years served as Johnson's "valet" — a not very demanding task!

King George, knowing how Johnson felt about America, hired him to write an anti-American pamphlet. Johnson accepted the assignment. The result was a pamphlet entitled *Taxation No Tryanny*.

It was so offensive that some passages had to be toned down before publication. But no amount of editing could transform it into a product worthy of the Johnson pen. When his friends read it, they felt great concern. In 1775 he was sixty-six years old. Had the combined effects of age and a multitude of bodily infirmities impaired his mental powers?

Actually some of his best writing was done in his later years. It was not because of the author's senility that *Taxation No Tyranny* was a shoddy job. It was shoddy because he didn't know much about his subject and was blinded by prejudice.

If there is anything favorable to be said about *Taxation No Tyranny*, it is that Johnson sincerely detested colonialism because it represented European exploitation of the natives. Also, he considered the American Congress hypocritical in appealing for abstract human rights while denying such rights to slaves. In writing this pamphlet, Johnson kept in mind Burke's *Speech on American Taxation*, delivered in 1774. (Burke, in turn, was answering the arguments in *Taxation No Tyranny* when he composed his speech *On Conciliation with the Colonies* in 1775.)

As a reward for writing *Taxation No Tyranny*, Johnson received an honorary degree of Doctor of Laws from Oxford University. It was not his first doctorate. In 1755 the university, where he had studied for only one year as an undergraduate, awarded him a doctorate for his work on his dictionary. In 1765 Trinity College, Dublin, awarded him the honorary degree of LL.D. It seems odd that he has gone down in history as "Dr. Johnson," since he himself never put on airs about his title. Boswell said that Johnson always referred to himself as "Mr. Johnson" and never used the title "Doctor."

While Johnson was writing *Taxation No Tyranny*, Burke was composing a speech that was to become the most famous of his speeches on behalf of the Americans.

On February 27, 1775, the House of Commons began to consider a bill to prevent New Englanders from using the Newfoundland fishing banks and from trading abroad except with Great Britain and the British West Indies. The purpose of the bill was to isolate New England and thus make it an example to the other colonies. It was certain to have a calamitous effect on New England. But British merchants would become the ultimate victims, since New Englanders would not be able to meet their financial obligations.

When Burke's Bristol constituents sent him a petition opposing the bill, he presented the petition to the House of Commons. But the administration assigned it to a committee Burke dryly termed the "Committee of Oblivion." Still, he did intend to have his say on the bill. On March 19 he conferred with Benjamin Franklin to get Franklin's help in selecting and supporting arguments to use against the Bill for Restraining the Trade and Commerce of New England.

On March 22, 1775, Burke stood up in the House of Commons at half-past three in the afternoon and began to deliver a speech that for generations to come would be a standard part of the curriculum in American schools. Today that speech is seldom taught in American public schools, but it is still regarded as a model of oratory. Some of the ideas expressed in that speech have become an important part of the American heritage.

Conciseness, usually considered a virtue in writing, was never characteristic of Burke. Like most of his speeches, this speech is very long. It fills 101 printed pages — enough to make a book in itself. It is dull in spots. In other spots the language is too florid. Yet some passages speed the pace of the heart like a band striking up a martial air.

One of the dull spots in the speech is the portion in which Burke presents statistics to show how enormously trade with the colonies had increased since the beginning of the century. But then he went on to dramatize those statistics:

Look at the manner in which the people of New England have of late carried on the whale fishery. Whilst we follow them among the tumbling mountains of ice, and behold them penetrating into the deepest frozen recesses of Hudson's Bay and Davis's Straits, whilst we are looking for them beneath the arctic circle, we hear that they have pierced into the opposite region of polar cold, that they are at the antipodes, and engaged under the frozen serpent of the south. Falkland, which seemed too remote and romantic an object for the grasp of national ambition, is but a stage and resting place in the progress of their victorious industry. Nor is the equatorial heat more discouraging to them than the accumulated winter of both the poles. We know that whilst some of them draw the line and strike the harpoon on the coast of Africa, others run the longitude, and pursue their gigantic game along the coast of Brazil. No sea but what is vexed by their fisheries, no climate that is not witness to their toils.

He objected to the use of force with the Americans on the ground that its effect was temporary and uncertain. Besides, those who used force were more likely to hurt themselves than their intended victims. He praised the spirit of the Americans and said that one reason for that spirit was the unusual kind of education that they had received:

In no country perhaps in the world is the law so general a study. The profession itself is numerous and in most provinces it takes the lead. The greater number of the deputies sent to the congress were lawyers. But all who read, and most do read, endeavour to obtain some smattering in that science. I have been told by an eminent bookseller that in no branch of his business, after tracts of popular devotion, were so many books as those on the law exported to the plantations. The colonists have now fallen into the way of printing them for their own use. I hear that they have sold nearly as many of "Blackstone's Commentaries" in America as in England. . . . This study renders men acute, inquisitive, dexterous, prompt in attack, ready to defence, full of resources. In other countries the people, more simple, and of a less mercurial cast, judge of an ill principle in government only by an actual grievance; here they anticipate the evil, and judge of the pressure of the grievances by the badness of the principle. They augur misgovernment at a distance and snuff the approach of tyranny in every tainted breeze.

His affection for the Americans, he said, grew

from common names, from kindred blood, from similar privileges, and equal protections. These are ties which, though light as air, are as strong as links of iron. Let the colonies always keep the idea of their civil rights associated with your government — they will cling and grapple to you; and no force under heaven will be of power to tear them from their allegiance. But let it be once understood, that your government may be one thing, and their privileges another; that these two things may exist without any mutual relation; the moment is gone; the cohesion is loosened; and everything hastens to decay and dissolution. As long as you have the wisdom to keep the sovereign authority of this country as the sanctuary of liberty, the sacred temple consecrated to our common faith, wherever the chosen race and sons of England worship freedom, they will turn their faces toward you. The more they multiply, the more perfect will be their obedience. Slavery they can have anywhere. It is a weed that grows in every soil. They may have it from Spain; they may have it from Prussia. But, until you become lost to all feeling of your true interest and your natural dignity, freedom they can have from none but you.

As he neared the end of his speech, he spoke the words that would one day be engraved beneath his statue in Washington, D.C: "Magnanimity in politics is not seldom the truest wisdom. . ."

The speech lasted for three hours. While Burke was speaking his brother Richard eavesdropped from the lobby of the House of Commons, occasionally going off for refreshment in a nearby coffeehouse. He was in the lobby when the speech ended. Then, he reported, he heard "the loudest, the most unanimous and the highest strain of applause."

But what the audience was applauding was the magnificence of the speech. The applause did not signify approval of Burke's proposals. He proposed thirteen resolutions, the general effect of which was to repeal the acts punishing Boston for the tea party and all acts imposing a duty on the colonists, to revert to the old system under which the colonial assemblies voted all internal taxes for the aid of the Crown. It was a great speech, but its timing was bad. The situation in the colonies was now so grave that something far more drastic was needed than a mere return to the old order.

But Burke had not expected his resolutions to carry. He had offered those resolutions because he felt an obligation to do so. The speech had not been a waste of time. He had influenced the minds of his countrymen and emphasized the importance of principle as a guide to conduct at a time when political corruption was rampant.

The Bill for Restraining the Trade and Commerce of New England was passed on March 30, 1775. Immediately King George began to sign commissions for generals and admirals. Regiments already stationed in the colonies must be reinforced without delay. News of the act did not reach America until early May.

But some who held commissions gave them up. The Earl of Effingham tore up his commission, saying, "I cannot without reproach from my own conscience consent to bear arms against my fellow-subjects in America in what, to my discernment, is not a clear cause." Lord Jeffrey Amherst refused to serve even when King George tried personally to persuade him. Amherst's chief reason for the refusal was that he feared he would not be given a sufficient number of troops for the difficult task. Since Amherst had served brilliantly in America during the Seven Years' War, he was well aware of the magnitude of such a task. The Earl of Chatham ordered his elder son, Lord Pitt, to resign his commission. James Wilson, an M.P. who was also a Captain of Marines, requested to lay down his commission, saying he could not, consistent with his own conscience, serve in the dispute against the Americans.

Late in May John Darby, captain of the schooner *Quero* from Salem, Massachusetts, arrived in London with a package of mail for Arthur Lee, agent for the Massachusetts Bay Colony. The package included copies of the *Essex Gazette,* dated April 25, which included a detailed account of the battle of Lexington and Concord on April 19. The front page of the newspaper was topped with a double row of coffins symbolizing the Americans who had died in that battle. Under the coffins was a screaming headline: "A BLOODY BUTCHERY BY THE KING'S TROOPS OR THE RUNAWAY FLIGHT OF THE REGULARS." Within twenty-four hours after Darby reached London, the news was spreading throughout England.

On May 28 Burke wrote to his friend Charles O'Hara, member of the Irish Parliament:

> All our prospects of American reconciliation are, I fear, over. The sluice is opened — Where, when, or how it will be stopped God only knows. A detachment was sent to destroy a Magazine which the Americans were forming at a Village called Concord. It proceeded with secrecy and dispatch. But the Americans were alert and conveyd their Stores, all told four pieces of Cannon and some flour, to a more distant Town called Worcester. The Country was not embodied; but they rose, without concert, order, or officers, and fell upon the Troops on their return. Lord Percy was sent out to sustain the first Party, which without his Assistance would, most certainly, never have returned. He too would have been defeated; if it had not been for two pieces of Artillery, which he had the precaution to take, and which were well served. The Troops behaved well; and retreated thirteen miles in pretty good order, it was a fatiguing day for them. Their loss did not exceed 70 killed; and probably about the same Number wounded. The

Provincials harassed them the whole way. Their loss was thirty-nine. During the time of this strange irregular engagement, which continued almost the whole of the day of the 19th of April, expresses were sent to every part of America with astonishing rapidity — and the whole Northern part of the continent was immediately under arms.

Burke's report is not entirely accurate, but all of the early reports of that battle contained some inaccuracies. For generations historians would analyze, almost minute by minute, what had actually happened that day. The important thing was that the Americans had had the audacity to fire on the king's troops. The boar had been driven too hard. It had turned on the hunter.

Only a few weeks after the battle of Lexington and Concord, a Second Continental Congress met in Philadelphia. On May 14, 1775, dining at the City Tavern, the delegates drank a toast to Edmund Burke for the speech he had delivered on March 22.

11. The Years After Lexington and Concord
(1775-1778)

TROUBLE HAD BEEN brewing in the colonies for so long that it was gratifying to have things come to a head. Burke was excited when he heard about Lexington and Concord — excited, but not elated. He had dreaded the prospect of war between England and the colonies. He had done all he could to prevent things from reaching that point. He still hoped that the conflict would be no more than a quick flare-up and that a reconciliation could be worked out. But so long as the war continued, he would follow its progress intently, sympathizing with the Americans and finding much to criticize in the behavior of many people in England.

After he heard about the battle of Bunker Hill (which occurred on June 17, 1775), he said:

No man commends the measures which have been pursued, or expects any good from those which are in preparation, but it is a cold, languid opinion, like what men discover in affairs that do not concern them . . . . The merchants are gone from us and from themselves . . . . The leading men among them are kept full fed with contracts and remittances and jobs of all descriptions, and are indefatigable in their endeavours to keep the others quiet . . . . They all, or the greatest number of them, begin to snuff the cadaverous *haut gout* of lucrative war. War has indeed become a sort of substitute for commerce. The freighting business never was so lively, on account of the prodigious taking up for transport service. Great orders for provisions and stores of all kinds . . . keep up the spirits of the mercantile world, and induce them to consider the American war not so much their calamity as their resource in inevitable distress.

These words have a modern ring. With few changes, they might have been said of war two centuries later. Now that the war had come, Burke read newspaper reports and letters from America with a feeling close to despair as he thought of the lives that were being lost, the ill-feeling that was being generated between two peoples of kindred blood. He couldn't bear to see people dancing in the streets at news of British victories. Victory for one side meant tragedy for the other side.

On November 12, 1775, he had a more personal cause for grief. His father-in-law died. Next day the following notice appeared in *The Public Advertiser*:

On Sunday Morning, died at his House in Suffolk-street, Christopher Nugent, Doctor of Physick, and Fellow of the Royal Society. He was an excellent Physician, a Man of general Erudition, of a most benevolent Temper, and a Friend to the Poor.

Many notes of condolence came to the Burke home, but probably none more heartfelt than the one Dr. Johnson sent to Jane. Johnson had been extremely fond of Nugent. Shortly after Nugent's death, when Johnson happened to see an omelet on the table, his massive frame shook in agony. The omelet reminded him of how Dr. Nugent, a devout Catholic, always ate an omelet on Fridays, when he was not allowed to eat meat. Johnson moaned, "Ah, my poor dear friend, I shall never eat omelet with thee again."

On November 16, 1775, Burke made another attempt to offer a plan for conciliation with the colonies in a bill providing that Parliament would not levy taxes upon the colonies except for the purpose of regulating trade and that revenue from customs duties would be at the disposal of colonial assemblies. The bill also provided that the American Congress would be authorized to legislate for the colonies. It would repeal some of the obnoxious acts and offer amnesty to Americans who had engaged in the war. This bill received more approbation than his previous proposals, but another three years would pass before the government was ready to offer the colonies the things that Burke proposed at this time.

Four days later Lord North proposed a bill prohibiting all commercial intercourse with the colonies. Since the bill was sure to pass, Burke did not resist it sharply, but he did try to have it slightly modified in a way that would benefit the merchants of Bristol.

Now that war had broken out, Johnson and Burke had a hard time avoiding the subject when they met. They did, for the sake of maintaining their friendship, steer around the subject when they were together, but each was well aware of what the other was saying to others. Johnson gloated over every American defeat. Burke was delighted at every American victory.

Still, Johnson had no great regard for the British military leaders. One day Boswell observed that Oliver Goldsmith had acquired more fame as a writer than had most of the officers in a recent campaign. Johnson said: "Why, Sir, you will find ten thousand fit to do what they did before you will find one who has done what Goldsmith has done."

In May, 1776, Boswell reported that he had found Burke in high spirits because word had just arrived in London about General George Washington's triumph in forcing General William Howe to evacuate Boston on March 17. No longer would the people of Boston have to watch the hated redcoats swaggering through their streets.

When, in August, Burke learned about the American Declaration of Independence, he accepted the fact that

Edmund Burke

Richard Burke (Edmund's son)

William Burke (Edmund's brother)

Mrs. Edmund Burke (née Jane Nugent)

Edmund Burke (left, white wig), 1765,
as secretary to the Marquess of Rockingham,
then Prime Minister

Burke's home, Gregories, Beaconsfield

William Pitt, first Earl of Chatham, 1772

William Pitt (the younger)

House of Commons, 1793

Hester Thrale

Fanny Burney

Dr. Samuel Johnson

Oliver Goldsmith

Sir Joshua Reynolds

James Boswell

Warren Hastings

America was lost to the British Empire. It would be wiser now, he thought, to grant the Americans their independence and relate to them as a friendly foreign nation than to prolong the war. Attempts to force the Americans to remain British subjects would never succeed. Even if defeated, the Americans would always resent the way they had been treated.

But the war was nowhere near its end. Burke would experience many days of grief as reports poured in of British victories in America. His deep distress over the suffering of the Americans is recorded in a letter he wrote on October 9, 1776, to Richard Champion, one of his Bristol constituents:

> Here is terrible news in town for the poor Americans. It would be a consolation if I could call it good for this Country. I have as yet heard it imperfectly. Three thousand of the Provincials are killed or prisoners. A total rout of all that were on Long Island, of which the King's troops are entire masters. They say they have burnt the camp and all on it, on account of the dirt and infectious filth of which it was full. They say further, that numbers were drowned on their flight to New York. The Provincials must evacuate that place; they say they are set upon by epidemical distempers. The number of the killed &c, on the Provincials' side is said to be three thousand; on the King's side three hundred Hessians, and not above fifty English.

In April he published *A Letter to the Sheriffs of Bristol on the Affairs of America,* one of his major writings on the American situation. In this letter he charged that the administration was proceeding on the false premise that America must be forced to surrender. This, he claimed, could no longer be expected. It would be wiser to make peace and allow the Americans to carry many points, "even some of them not quite reasonable," than to run the risk that the Americans might turn for aid to England's old enemies, France and Spain. He called for immediate repeal of all acts concerning America which had been passed since 1763. If this were done, he suggested, the Americans might not insist on their independence. But even if they did, American independence without war was preferable to American independence with war.

Commenting on the fight that the Americans had been making for their rights, he said:

> We cannot, midst the excesses and abuses which have happened, help respecting the spirit and principles operating in these commotions. The principles bear so close a resemblance to those which support the most valuable part of our constitution, that we cannot think of extirpating them in any part of His Majesty's dominions, without admitting consequences, and establishing precedents, the most dangerous to the liberties of this kingdom.

He attacked the war zealots, those to whom war was profitable:

> I cannot conceive any existence under heaven (which, in the depths of its wisdom, tolerates all sorts of things) that is more truly odious and disgusting, than an impotent helpless creature, without civil wisdom or military skill, without a consciousness of any other qualifications for power but his servility to it, bloated with pride and arrogance, calling for battles which he is not to fight, contending for a violent dominion which he can never exercise, and satisfied to be himself mean and miserable, in order to render others contemptible and wretched. The addressers offer their own persons, and they are satisfied with hiring Germans. They promise their private fortunes, and they mortgage their country. They have all the merit of volunteers, without risk of person or charge of contribution; and when the unfeeling arm of a foreign soldiery pours out their kindred blood like water, they exult and triumph as if they themselves had performed some notable exploit.

Because it was impossible to raise enough British troops, King George had hired Hessian soldiers from Germany.

These troops now constituted approximately one-third of the troops in America.

Burke concluded the letter with a passage expressing his views on civil liberty:

> The *extreme* of liberty (which is its abstract perfection, but its real fault) obtains nowhere nor ought to obtain anywhere, because extremes, as we all know, in every point which relates either to our duties or satisfactions in life, are destructive both to virtue and enjoyment. Liberty, too, must be limited in order to be possessed. The degree of restraint it is impossible in any case to settle precisely. But it ought to be the constant aim of every wise public counsel to find out by cautious experiments, and rational, cool endeavours, with how little, not how much, of this restraint the community can subsist; for liberty is a good to be improved, and not an evil to be lessened.

This letter was Burke's last formal discourse on the American situation.

The surrender of Burgoyne at Saratoga on October 17, 1777, led to such sharp criticism of British policy that it nearly resulted in the end of the war. On December 2 news of the defeat reached London. Next day several members of the House of Commons spoke in Burgoyne's defense and blamed the disaster on the incompetent Lord George Germain, Minister of War. Germain had a serious blemish on his record. People had not forgotten that he was dismissed as a field officer in 1759 for failing to obey orders. Such a disgrace might have ruined most men. But Germain came from a family with enormous political clout. Not only did he suffer no permanent disgrace, but he was eventually appointed to his present position, where he attempted to command an army three thousand miles away.

It wasn't fair to lay all the blame on Germain for the Saratoga disaster. Burgoyne was not entirely blameless for his surrender to the "cowardly colonial rabble." But Burgoyne, handsomest man in the British army, had tremendous charm (he was known as "Gentlemen Johnny"). He had many friends in Parliament. Now those friends, including Burke, stood up to speak of him flatteringly. After praising Burgoyne's courage and skill, Burke savagely censured Germain, then turned on Attorney-General Wedderburn, whom he described as "counsel" to Germain. Wedderburn hotly defended himself, and Burke let out a derisive laugh. Wedderburn was so infuriated that he offered to give Burke "a lesson in manners." Burke walked out of the house, pausing at the door, where he beckoned Wedderburn to follow him. Other members, fearing that a duel would result, managed to calm both men down, at least temporarily.

The public charge that he needed a lesson in manners cut Burke deeply. His manners, he knew, lacked the polish of those who had been born to higher station. Sometimes he did behave crudely. The hurts and snubs of a lifetime were simmering inside him by the time he got home. There he dashed off an insulting note to Wedderburn. Then, reconsidering, he tore it up and wrote an icily polite letter in which he asked whether Wedderburn had meant to threaten him. Wedderburn replied to the note immediately, saying that he had intended no threat.

Rockingham's affection for Burke is touchingly revealed in a note he sent Burke at midnight, expressing his relief that there was to be no duel:

My dear Burke

> My Heart is at Ease
> ever yours
> most affectly
> Rockingham

On December 5, 1777, David Hartley in the House of Commons moved a series of resolutions against further prosecution of the American war. In the debate that followed, those who supported the resolutions argued that France might join America if the war continued. But the resolutions were not carried. Too many members wanted to carry on a war they were sure would end with victory for England.

While this debate was in progress, Benjamin Franklin was in Paris, working on French fears that Burgoyne's surrender might lead Lord North to offer the Americans generous peace terms provided the Americans would agree to return to the British Empire. The French people were elated over the news of the American victory at Saratoga. Now they demanded war with England. France would at long last get revenge for the humiliations inflicted on her at the end of the Seven Years' War. On December 6 King Louis XVI recognized the independence of the young United States of America. And Franklin had little difficulty in persuading the French to ally themselves with the Americans. On February 6, 1778, France signed two treaties with the United States, one of amity and commerce, one of alliance.

On the same day and before news of the treaties had reached England, Burke delivered a speech in the House of Commons, protesting against the use of Indians in warfare. During the Seven Years' War both French and English commanders had used Indians as scouts for exploring the woods. But they had never used Indians in combat except to attack an armed foe. Lord North and his colleagues were the first to authorize the use of Indians to attack defenseless civilians. Bribed with double rations of food and brandy, Indians had been turned loose upon peaceful American communities. They had slaughtered women and children, the aged and the helpless. The tortures they had inflicted were too hideous to be described in accounts intended for the general public.

But Burke, in letters from America, had accumulated a mass of information about such atrocities. And he spared his audience no gory detail. Tears rolled down the cheeks of his listeners. Later some of them expressed relief that the galleries were closed to visitors while Burke was speaking. If members of the public had heard what he had to say, they might have physically assaulted the ministers who had condoned such cruelty.

Humor was not Burke's strong suit, and his subject was as unfunny as a subject could be. But one portion of this speech was so hilarious that his audience was convulsed. Even Prime Minister North, who usually napped at his desk, did no dozing at that point in the speech where Burke parodied Burgoyne's instructions to the Indians. North laughed so hard that his face turned purple.

Burgoyne had addressed the Indians in such words as these: "The clemency of your father (King George) has been abused, the offers of his mercy have been despised, and his further patience would, in his eyes, become culpable, inasmuch as it would withhold redress from the most grievous oppressions in the province that ever disgraced the history of mankind."

Burgoyne then invited the Indians — who, of course, had given careful consideration to the right of taxation inherent in Parliament — to rally around His Majesty's standard, tomahawks in hand. He cautioned them not to touch a hair on the head of man, woman, or child while living, but said that he would pay handsomely for the scalps of the dead. He would have no difficulty, of course, in distinguishing between scalps taken from those already dead and those who had died of being scalped. Burgoyne's speech was so absurdly high-falutin that the interpreter couldn't possibly make it intelligible to the Indians, who represented seventeen tribes speaking different dialects.

To show how absurd Burgoyne's instructions were, Burke indicated how the keeper of His Majesty's zoo might instruct the animals before sending them out to quell a riot in the city: "My gentle lions, my humane bears, my sentimental wolves, my tender-hearted hyenas, go forth against the seditious mob on your mission of oppression and retribution; but I exhort you, as you are Christians, and members of a civilized society, to take care not to hurt man, woman, or child."

When the House of Commons convened on February 17, 1778, Lord North delivered an address in which he revealed an astonishing change of heart toward the Americans. He said that the Cabinet had resolved to abandon the tea duty, to renounce the power of taxing America without her consent, to repeal the Boston Port Acts, the Massachusetts Government Act, and the Act for Restraining the Trade and Commerce of New England. He was now ready to recognize the Continental Congress and the virtual independence of America within the framework of the British Empire. These concessions, he insisted, had been made "from reason and propriety, not from necessity."

Charles Fox, a young member who had become a close friend of Burke's, listened politely until North reached the end of his speech. Then Fox stood up and sarcastically congratulated North for joining the opposition. Suddenly he changed his tone and sharply demanded to know whether America had already signed a treaty with France.

North was too stunned to speak. His bulging eyes looked stricken. His lips trembled but were unable to form words. Several other members demanded an answer to Fox's question. Finally North struggled to his feet and lamely admitted that he had heard a rumor about such a treaty. The truth was that a copy of the treaty lay on his desk at that moment. But he couldn't bring himself to say so. He couldn't admit that it was indeed "dire necessity" that had driven him to become generous to the Americans.

North's behavior in this situation shows him in an unfavorable light, as indeed, do most of his dealings with the American colonists. Yet those who knew him personally found him to be a man of considerable charm, with a keenness of intellect belied by his air of being unconcerned with what happened around him and his unprepossessing physical appearance. He had puffy cheeks and a flabby dewlap, and his bulging heavy-lidded eyes gave him (as Horace Walpole put it) "the air of a blind trumpeter." While Burke or some other long-winded speaker was fulminating, he would sit with his feet on the Treasury Bench, looking as if he were wool-gathering. But when the speaker finished, his sharp reply would show that he hadn't missed a trick.

Burke actually liked and admired North more than a little. He once said of North: "He was a man of admirable parts, of general knowledge, of a versatile understanding, fitted for all sorts of business; of infinite wit and pleasantry, of a delightful temper, and with a mind most disinterested." But Burke did add that North lacked "something of the vigilance and spirit of command that the time required."

12. The War Continues
(1778-1779)

NOW THERE WAS no denying that England was on the brink of war with France. Not only that, but France enjoyed a tremendous advantage. After nearly three years of war with America, the English fleet had started to disintegrate. And France had been strengthening her navy during the fifteen years since the end of the Seven Years' War.

Burke and his friends in Parliament urged the administration to make peace with America immediately. But they were strongly opposed by those who were determined to bring the Americans to their knees. .

The Earl of Chatham, former Prime Minister William Pitt, had long differed with Burke on how to handle the American situation. Now Chatham was infuriated that the pro-American M.P.'s wanted to give up America without a struggle. Although he was now nearly seventy and so feeble that he could not walk unaided, he was determined to fight with his last breath to hold on to America. On April 7, 1778, he tottered into the House of Lords, leaning on crutches and supported on either side by his son, the younger William Pitt, and his son-in-law, Lord Mahon. The deathly pallor of Chatham's face was accentuated by his suit of black velvet.

As he came through the door, everyone stood up in tribute to him. He nodded solemnly. Then slowly and painfully, he made his way to a seat at the front of the room. With the two young men still supporting him, he started to speak. But his voice had little strength. Some of his sentences were incoherent, and his train of thought was hard to follow. But as he went on he seemed to acquire more force. Some passages of the speech were as brilliant as any that he had ever uttered.

> I am risen from my bed to stand up in the cause of my country, perhaps never again to speak in this house. I have made an effort, almost beyond my strength, to come here today to express my indignation at an idea which has gone forth of yielding up America. My lords, I rejoice that the grave has not closed upon me, that I am still alive to lift up my voice against the dismemberment of this ancient and noble monarchy. Pressed down, as I am, by the needs of infirmity, I am little able to assist my country in this most perilous conjuncture; but, my lords, whilst I have sense and memory I will never consent to deprive the royal offspring of the house of Brunswick of their fairest inheritance . . . . Shall we tarnish the lustre of this nation by an ignominious surrender of its rights and fairest possessions? Shall this great kingdom, which has survived whole and entire Danish predations, the Scottish inroads, and the Norman conquest — that has stood the threatened invasion of the Spanish Armada — now fall prostrate before the house of Bourbon?
>
> My lords, any state is better than despair. Let us at least make an effort, and, if we must fall, let us fall like men. My lords, ill as I am, yet so long as I can crawl down to this house, and have strength to raise myself on my crutches, or lift my head, I will vote against giving up the dependency of America on the sovereignty of Great Britain, and if no other lord is of opinion with me. I will protest against the measure.

Suddenly he fell back in his seat, gasping and clutching his throat. Everyone jumped up and hurried around, some running for medical assistance, some producing flasks of brandy. Within a few minutes Chatham was placed on a stretcher and carried out of the house. His death was expected momentarily, but he clung to life for several weeks.

On May 13, at his estate in Kent, he drew his last breath. His son William, who was only nineteen at the time, was seated at his bedside, reading from Homer the scene of Hector's funeral and the despair of Troy.

King George had long been at odds with Chatham. Now he was petty enough to oppose a plan for a monument to be erected in Chatham's honor. But the House of Commons voted for a public funeral and a monument and also granted a generous sum to the bereaved family. Burke had been no friend of Chatham in recent years, and had in fact made unkind remarks about him even after his collapse, so it was probably rather hypocritical of Burke to agree to serve as a pallbearer. And the inscription that Burke later composed for the monument erected to Chatham at the Guildhall did not single out Chatham for special mention, but simply implied that he had been a great man: "The means by which Providence raises a nation to greatness are the virtues infused in its great men."

The American crisis was now taking up so much of Burke's time that he rarely attended meetings of the Club. But the death of a Club member always brought the members together. When David Garrick died, on January 20, 1779, the members indulged in their customary expressions of respect and admiration. Dr. Johnson uttered one of the most famous epitaphs in history: "I am disappointed by that stroke of death which has eclipsed the gaiety of nations and impoverished the subtle stock of harmless pleasure." On February 1 the Club attended Garrick's funeral at Westminster Abbey. As Burke stood by the actor's burial place, he remarked: "The spot was well chosen, for the statue of Shakespeare seems to point to the grave where the great actor of his works is laid."

The early months of 1779 were among the most critical of the war. After the French became the allies of the colonists, they aided in the war effort, not only in America, but in faraway India as well. English communication with India was in constant danger, and, at least once, it was cut off entirely. French fleets sailed to Indian waters. French troops landed on Indian soil. The British position in India became precarious. And now, when it seemed possible that the American colonies might actually be lost, the value of India to the British Empire was enormously enhanced. No businessman in Britain could fail to perceive that the American Revolution was threatening to swing the entire balance of British trade over to the East.

The situation closer to home was even worse. Vessels flying the French and American flags were prowling in the English Channel, and the British fleet was too weak to risk an engagement. And in Ireland the threat of revolution had become menacing. Coastal areas in Ireland and Scotland were under constant alarm by audacious attacks from American vessels, but England lacked frigates to guard against such attacks.

In June, 1779, Spain declared war on England. Now the likelihood of a combined Spanish-French invasion became acute. England was appallingly unprepared to resist an invasion. Most of her ships were now in American waters. And there weren't nearly enough shipwrights in England to build the ships that would be needed to forestall an invasion. Furthermore, the supply of seamen needed to man such ships was critically low.

That summer Burke became so depressed over the way the enemy fleets were domineering over the English that he wrote to Richard Champion:

> I am low and dejected at times in a way not to be described. . .I cannot look our present situation steadily in the face; and everything in prospect appears to me so very gloomy that I am willing to turn to any sort of trifling amusement which has a tendency to avert my mind from all speculation upon evils which no thoughts of mine at all avert or lessen.

The situation seemed so desperate that Richard Champion, Burke's Bristol friend, invited Jane Burke to stay at his home, since the west coast of England was likely to be safer than the east coast. Burke declined the offer a bit melo-dramatically, saying that he intended to remain in London to fight for his life and for his country in case the invaders should arrive.

Meanwhile the Irish Parliament, impatient with a British administration that seemed unconcerned about Ireland, took advantage of the situation to cut off all commerce with England. Unofficially, the Irish had raised a 40,000-man citizen army, the Irish Volunteers. This army professed to be a national guard to protect Ireland against invasion. In fact, it was a weapon of political threat against England.

For years Burke and his friends had been arguing that trading regulations should be modified to give the Irish a fair share in the profits. But English merchants, fearing that anything gained by the Irish would mean a loss for themselves, had bombarded Parliament with petitions. Lord North was so intimidated by such petitions that he and his supporters watered down bills proposed by the Rocking-hams.

But on November 15, 1779, riots broke out in the streets of Dublin. And a rumor circulated that the Irish were planning a rebellion based on lessons learned from the Americans. Now that Lord North's back was against the wall, he decided to be generous to Ireland. On December 12, 1779, he proposed bills permitting the free import of wools, woolens, and glass from Ireland and opening the trade of the empire to Ireland.

Burke was disgusted at seeing North take all the credit for aiding Ireland. For many years Burke had been concerned about the plight of Ireland. His letters to Irish friends over the years indicate that he had done what he could for Ireland. But North's bills now asked for things that Burke had been asking for all along. Besides, Burke had a very bad cold at the time and was so hoarse that he could hardly speak. He sat back quietly while the debates on North's bills were in progress. Since the administration supported those bills and since the opposition would certainly not object to them, nothing Burke might have said would have made any significant difference.

After the bills were passed, the Irish praised North for his generosity and abused Burke. Some went so far as to charge that Burke had remained silent during the debate for fear of offending British merchants. Burke was so incensed that he wrote a long letter on January 1, 1780, to Thomas Burgh, a friend in Ireland, explaining how hard and long he had worked on Ireland's behalf. Burke asked Burgh to show the letter to influential people in Ireland. Burgh did so and said that the letter had done some good. But Burke could never completely forgive his Irish friends for their short memories and lack of faith in him.

Just before the Christmas recess in 1779 Burke announced he intended to present a plan that would not only abolish royal corruption but would strengthen the state and thus promote the survival of the British Empire. On February 11, 1780, before packed galleries and a crowded house, he asked permission to bring in his Bill for the Reformation of Civil Establishments. The vote to grant such permission just missed being unanimous. There was only one dissenter — Lord George Gordon, a crackpot aristocrat who detested Burke for having supported the rights of Catholics. According to a clumsy arrangement, the ayes were required to go out to the lobby, while the noes kept their seats to have their votes counted. Thus everyone except Gordon swarmed into the small lobby, while he sat alone in the house.

Burke then proceeded to deliver a speech so magnificent that even his opponents admired it. He wanted to reduce expenditures and eliminate corrupt influence, he said. The king's court had "lost all that was stately and venerable in the antique manners, without retrenching any of the cumbrous charge of a Gothic establishment." The royal household included a multitude of offices, many of which had been established during the Middle Ages and now served no purpose except to "keep alive corrupt hope and servile dependence."

Every branch of the internal administration of the royal palace was ridiculously overmanned. Except for the most menial servants, who were overworked, everyone was underworked or did nothing more strenuous than picking up a salary. The royal wardrobe, to mention one of many possible examples, was in the charge of the Master of the Robes, the Keeper of the Wardrobe, the Keeper of the Removing Wardrobe, the Groom of the Stole, the King's Valet, and the King's Valet's Deputy. But the only one who knew the contents of the wardrobe was the King's Valet's Deputy.

Menial servants and tradesmen went unpaid for months or even years. Those who simply sat around holding titles claimed all the benefits that went with those titles. Twenty-three separate tables were laid each day in various apartments of the palace for those who considered themselves entitled to free meals. Yet those same persons also pocketed money that had been allotted to them to pay for their meals. Money that should have gone to pay the butcher, the grocer, or the coachmaker was used to buy the votes of Members of Parliament, to corrupt the daily press, to persecute authors and printers of pamphlets offensive to the king.

Burke's speech sparkled with fascinating details of the way in which money was being squandered — and at a time when money was badly needed for the defense of the nation. His audience was spellbound while he was speaking. When he finished, his friend Charles Fox rose and doffed his hat in tribute as he seconded Burke's motion for a resolution to bring about economic reform. But the opponents of the plan resorted to every possible ruse to delay a vote. They referred the bill to a committee, which slashed it to shreds. A few of Burke's minor proposals were accepted, but all of the significant proposals were argued away. Nevertheless, his suggestions for reform were introduced again a few years later, and some of his more important proposals were approved. The present British civil service system has its roots in proposals originally made by Burke.

13. The Gordon Riots
(1780)

IT IS EASY TO understand why Burke had a warm spot in his heart for Catholics — he had so many Catholic relatives. And the fact that he attended a Quaker school undoubtedly helped to make him more religiously tolerant than most men of his time. Quakers had suffered severely from persecution for decades after the founding of their religious group (formally called the "Society of Friends") in the middle of the seventeenth century. Quakers were — and to this day are — known for their tolerant attitude toward those whose faith differs from their own. But "tolerant" is not the best word to describe Burke's attitude. That word smacks a bit of condescension, a feeling that one's own faith is the best or the only correct one, but that others have a right to hold different beliefs. Burke's appreciation of religious faiths went beyond this smug kind of tolerance. His attitude is best expressed in his words:

> I would give a full civic protection, in which I include an immunity from all disturbance of the public religious worship, and a power of teaching in schools as well as temples, to Jews, Mahometans, and even Pagans; especially if they are already possessed of those advantages by long and prescriptive usage, which is as sacred in this exercise of rights, as in any others.

His concern for the plight of Catholics must have begun long before he was old enough to understand the distinctions between one religious faith and another. Even though his Catholic relatives in Ballyduff would never have tried to convert him to their own faith, he must have heard references to the mistreatment of Catholics when he was no older than six. And he observed, as he grew older, that many Irish Protestants never conversed with Catholics. Some Protestants found Catholics so repulsive that they wouldn't hire them to work even in their stables. In England he had found that there were still Protestants who could express horror at the persecution of Huguenots under Louis XIV; yet those same persons persecuted their Catholic neighbors with a misery quite as intense and possibly more degrading. Fighting this type of prejudice was almost impossibly difficult. It would have been pointless to introduce a bill in the House of Commons for the relief of Catholics, since it would have had no chance of passing.

Not until 1778, when he was forty-nine years old, did he find an opportunity to bring about a few changes in legislation affecting Catholics. Then it was because it was expedient at that time to grant Catholics a few privileges so that they might aid in the war effort. Charles Carroll of Maryland had been luring Irish Catholics to America by offering them land and religious freedom. Some of those Irishmen might join the Continental Army to fight against their English oppressors. Besides, many M.P.'s owned land in Ireland. The value of that property might decline as more and more Irishmen left for America instead of working for starvation wages in Ireland.

Burke took advantage of the situation to draft a Catholic Relief Bill. Because his enemies had played up his Catholic background, it seemed unwise for him to introduce the bill himself. The bill was therefore sponsored by Sir George Savile. It was not as strong as Burke would have liked. To assure passage, he had to ask for what he was likely to get. Both Houses of Parliament passed the bill, and King George signed it on June 3, 1778.

The Catholic Relief Bill made it easier for Catholics to purchase and inherit land. It allowed Catholic clergy and teachers to perform their vocations without risking life imprisonment. It allowed Catholics to worship in their own way, but required them to take an oath denying the temporal power of the Pope. It did not, however, remove all restrictions from Catholics. They were still, for instance, denied the right to hold political office. And the law applied only to England. As had been expected, though, the Irish Parliament quickly passed a similar bill.

In gratitude to Burke for this great step forward in alleviating the miseries of Catholics, the Catholic Association of Ireland offered him a gift of a hundred guineas. As usual, he was head over heels in debt, but he declined the gift and asked that the money be used to educate Irish Catholic youth.

The Speaker of the Irish House of Commons wrote to Burke: "On this happy event I sincerely congratulate you, being fully persuaded that it is of more real importance to our country than any law that has been passed during my time."

To King George's credit, it must be said that he tolerated religious dissension. He had protected the Quakers, the Methodists, and all other sects in their freedom of worship. He disliked Roman Catholicism, but he did wish to relieve the sufferings of Catholics. After signing the Catholic Relief Bill, he asked Parliament to introduce another bill for the relief of Catholics in Scotland.

Anti-Catholic sentiment was much stronger in Scotland than in England. The zealots of the kirk expressed their resentment by pillaging Catholic homes, setting fire to Catholic chapels, instigating riots. Terrified Catholics in Scotland wrote to Burke, begging for protection. He presented their petition to the House of Commons on March 12, 1779. Commons took no action. But Lord George Gordon, member of the Scottish nobility, was enraged that Burke should have presumed to introduce such a petition.

Gordon had entered the House of Commons in 1775, representing the pocket borough of Luggershall in Wiltshire. In 1780 he was twenty-nine years old, tall and lean, with long black hair falling to his shoulders. His face was pale and tense. Whenever he spoke of Catholics, his eyes blazed with maniacal fury.

Now he aroused the Scots by distributing hate-mongering handbills and posters and by making speeches. Late in 1779 he was elected President of the Protestant Association of England. He induced that association to petition for repeal of the Catholic Relief Act. On January 4, 1780, he called on Lord North at 10 Downing Street and handed him the petition. When North refused to accept it, Gordon threatened North and those responsible for the Catholic Relief Act.

Since Gordon was enormously wealthy, he had the power to carry out his threat. He managed to get a hundred thousand signatures on sheets of parchment, then had a tailor stitch the sheets together to form a gigantic scroll. He then placed advertisements in the newspapers, directing his supporters to gather at St. George's Fields on June 2, wearing blue cockades in their hats. He would not present the petition to Parliament, he said, unless at least twenty thousand followers marched with him to Parliament.

On the morning of June 2 more than sixty thousand showed up at St. George's Fields. Section leaders started them marching around, holding blue flags aloft. Scotsmen skirled bagpipes. The marchers shouted "No Popery!" Around noon a man arrived, carrying the huge scroll of signatures. Led by Lord Gordon, the marchers headed for Parliament.

There they forced their way into the lobby. Those who couldn't get inside attacked M.P.'s who were trying to enter the building. The demonstrators dragged drivers and footmen from the carriages and rolled them in the mud. Somebody yanked Lord North's hat off his head, ripped the hat into pieces, and proceeded to sell the pieces for a

shilling apiece. By the time the M.P.'s joined their colleagues who were already inside the building, they had
been stripped half naked. Their mud-smeared clothes
hung in tatters, their wigs had been knocked off, their
bodies were bruised and bleeding. The air vibrated with the
sound of carriages being shattered, the roar of the mob, the
cries of the victims. A kinsman of Lord Gordon, General
James Murray, warned him that if one of his rascally adher-
ents dared to enter the House, "I will plunge my sword, not
into his, but into your body."

When Gordon presented his petition in the House of
Commons, he was dumbfounded to find that only eight
members supported his motion for repeal of the Catholic
Relief Act. What could he do now? He couldn't tell his
followers that their show of force had accomplished so
little. Yet he was shrewd enough to know that he'd better
not stir up further violence. If he did, he could be charged
with treason. He went to the outer gallery of the House and
told the crowd in the courtyard that the king would surely
grant their wishes. "When he hears that the people ten
miles around are collecting, there is no doubt that he will
send his ministers private orders to repeal." Then he
warned the crowd against evil persons who might try to
"incite mischief." Having said this, he had washed his
hands of blame for the disorders that were certain to ensue.

From time to time he returned to the gallery and ranted
about those who had supported the Catholic Relief Act.
Every time he mentioned such names as Edmund Burke or
Sir George Savile, the mob roared. The roaring went on for
hours while the M.P.'s inside the building remained prisoners, unable to leave the building without risking their
lives. By eleven o'clock at night the crowd had melted
away. Then the M.P.'s left, riding six to a carriage, hands
on sword hilts.

When Burke got home (to a house he kept in London), he
stored his books and papers in a safe place. Then he
dismissed the sixteen soldiers whom the government had

sent to protect him, saying, "I think that, with the scarcity of troops, you might be better employed than in looking after my paltry remains." His barber, an Irish Catholic who was devoted to him, came to say that he had "a handful of staunch-hearted native lads in the next public house" who wanted to serve as Burke's bodyguards. Burke declined the offer. He and his wife went to the home of their friend, General John Burgoyne, who had returned to England in 1778 as a prisoner on parole. Burke left Jane in Burgoyne's care, then went to help defend Lord Rockingham's London home.

Lord Jeffrey Amherst, commander-in-chief of the forces of the nation, asked for authority to use troops against the mob. But Secretary of War Jenkinson said that troops could not legally intervene until a civil magistrate instructed them to do so. They could not fire until the riot act had been read publicly and the mob given an hour to disperse.

On the night of June 2 a mob broke into the Sardinian and Bavarian embassies, which contained chapels for Roman Catholic services. They stole costly chalices and vestments and demolished pulpits and pews.

On the evening of June 3 a mob poured into a district where many Irish Catholics lived. One Irish merchant appealed to the Lord Mayor of London for protection, but the Lord Mayor said that he could not interfere, because there were "very great people at the bottom of the riot."

The Lord Mayor had won his office because of his wealth. He had no other qualifications. He had started as a waiter in a tavern and cultivated friendships with crooks, eventually becoming a rich merchant. Since he despised M.P.'s, he was having the time of his life watching the riots.

On Sunday, June 4, the mob smashed windows in a Catholic chapel in the Irish district, then set fire to the chapel. The Lord Mayor looked on until the fire had done appalling damage, then said, "That's pretty well, gentlemen, for one evening. I hope you will now go to your homes."

On June 5 the rioters demolished another Catholic chapel, a Catholic seminary, and the homes of many Irish Catholics. Then they pillaged the home of Sir George Savile, sponsor of the Catholic Relief Act.

On June 6 the streets were thronged with people wearing blue cockades. Burke walked through the crowd on his way to the House of Commons, aware that everyone knew who he was. At one point two men threatened him. He drew his sword, saying, "If you want me, here I am, but never expect that I shall vote for repeal of the act I supported." At this someone cried, "He's a gentleman, make way for him." Some men wearing blue cockades actually wished him well. He reached the House of Commons safely. There he delivered a three-hour speech, denouncing the rioters and demanding action to suppress the tumults.

That evening the rioters, armed with pickaxes and sledgehammers, battered down the gates of Newgate Prison and dragged the prisoners out of their cells. Then they set fire to the prison and surged on to attack Clerkenwell and Brideswell Prisons.

One eyewitness to the attack on Newgate Prison said:

They broke the roof, tore away the rafters, and, having got ladders, they descended. Not Orpheus himself had more courage or better luck. Flames all round them and a body of soldiers expected, they defied and laughed at all opposition. The prisoners escaped, I stood and saw about twelve women and eight men ascend from their confinement to the open air, and they were conducted through the street in their chains. Three of these were to be hanged on Friday. You have no conception of the frenzy of the multitude. . . . With some difficulty, they then fired the debtors' prison, broke the doors, and they too all made their escape.

A member of the House of Commons, Nathaniel Wraxall, recorded a scene he witnessed that same evening:

. . .Quitting the coach, we crossed the square, and had scarcely got under the wall of Bedford House, when we heard the door of Lord Mansfield's house burst open with violence. In a few minutes, all the contents of the apartments being precipitated from the windows, were piled up and wrapped in flames. A file of foot soldiers arriving, drew up near the blazing pile, but without either attempting to quench the fire or to impede the mob, who were indeed far too numerous to admit of being dispersed, or even intimidated, by a small detachment of infantry.

On the morning of June 7 Lord Gordon asked for an audience with the king, who was meeting with his Cabinet members. Oddly — in view of the fact that the king had been complaining because Gordon was still at large — Gordon was not arrested. Instead, the king wrote a note saying: "It is impossible for the king to see Lord Gordon until he has given sufficient proof of his allegiance and loyalty by employing those means which, he says, he has in his power to quell the disturbances and restore order to this capital."

Lord Rockingham was late in arriving at this Cabinet meeting. When he did arrive, he was trembling with fury. For five nights, with the assistance of Burke and other friends, he had defended his home against the rioters. Now he asked indignantly why the mob had not been dispersed by force.

Until this moment the king had assumed that he lacked the legal power to take action without the cooperation of the civil magistrates. Now he consulted Attorney-General Wedderburn, who said that common law protecting citizens and their property superseded any law having to do with unlawful assembly.

Immediately the king sent word to Lord Amherst that his troops could now shoot at the mob. Then he issued a proclamation in which he instructed the military to use force. The proclamation was read aloud in various parts of the city, but most of the rioters failed to hear it. Believing that the troops wouldn't dare to fire, those rioters went on with their work of destruction.

On the night of June 7 a mob set fire to Langdale's distillery, which was owned by a Catholic. Thousands of people swarmed in from slummy alleys, eager to get free liquor while the vats were being demolished. They rushed down to the cellars to fill pots, jugs, pig troughs. Some knelt in the streets to gulp down the brew flowing through the gutters. Suddenly sheets of fire swept across the alcoholic river. The looters became living torches. Near midnight a mob advanced on the Bank of England, which was heavily guarded with troops. Lord Gordon showed up and told the captain of the troops that he could disperse the mob. The captain looked at Gordon coldly, then ordered his troops to fire. A second later eight persons lay dead. Others were moaning from wounds. The soldiers then charged into the crowd with bayonets.

Meanwhile, through smoke-reeking streets, came the sound of soldiers' boots and the rattle of musketry. Regiments were arriving from all parts of England.

Before dawn the Bank of England had been freshly whitewashed and was ready for normal business. Soldiers went through the streets tearing "No Popery" signs off shopdoors, pulling blue cockades from hats. Released felons, some with chains still dangling from their legs, wandered aimlessly about. Most of them had no home but prison. Makeshift shelters had to be built for them. A sickly quiet came over the city. The stench of burnt human flesh filled the air. Smoke rose from the remains of fires.

No accurate estimate could be made of the number of persons who lost their lives during the riots. Countless bodies were consumed in flames. Soldiers killed about two hundred. Crowds fleeing across bridges crushed many to death and pushed others into the river. Many of the wounded died within a few days after the riots ended. Others died from the effects of drinking raw alcohol. The death toll may well have been more than eight hundred. Horace Walpole, in his *Memoirs*, described "Black Wednesday" (June 7) as "the most horrible night I ever beheld, which for six hours together I expected to end in half the town being reduced to ashes.''

Several other prominent Londoners left reports in diaries or letters. Samuel Johnson, standing at the windows of his study at Bolt Court, was appalled. He said, ''One might see the glare of conflagration fill the sky from many parts; the sight was dreadful.''

And Mrs. Thrale, in a long letter to her sister Fanny, assured her that

> . . .we are pretty quiet and tranquil again now. Papa goes on with his business pretty much as usual, and so far from the military keeping people within doors (as you say, in your letter to my father, you suppose to be the case), the streets were never more crowded — everybody is wandering about in order to see the ruins of the places that the mob have destroyed.
>
> There are two camps, one in St. James's, and the other in Hyde Park, which, together with the military law, makes almost everyone here think he is safe again. I expect we shall all have ''a passion for a scarlet coat'' now. I hardly know what to tell you that won't be stale news. They say that duplicates of the handbill that I have enclosed were distributed all over the town on Wednesday and Thursday; however, thank Heaven, everybody says now that Mr. Thrale's house and brewery are as safe as we can wish them. There was a brewer in Turnstile that had his house gutted and burnt, because, the mob said, ''he was such a popish, and sold popish beer.'' Did you ever hear of such diabolical ruffians?. . .

Edward Gibbon, author of *The History of the Decline and Fall of the Roman Empire,* said: ''Our disgrace will be lasting, and the month of June 1780, will ever be marked by a dark and diabolical fanaticism which I had supposed to be extinct.''

14. The War Ends
(1780-1781)

MOST OF THOSE who died in the Gordon Riots were obscure poor people. But hardly anyone, however high his station, could have been sure that his own life and property would be spared. The mob attacked the homes of several aristocrats, but avoided the homes of those who had opposed the Catholic Relief Act. They also spared the home of Lord Jeffrey Amherst, perhaps realizing that he would give orders to shoot if he were personally attacked. And they did not go near the royal palace. Uncontrolled though the rioters were and much as they may have disapproved of some of the actions of the king, they still felt too much awe at his power to attack him or any of the royal residences.

Richard Shackleton, with good reason, worried about Burke during the riots, since Burke was the person chiefly responsible for the Catholic Relief Act. Shackleton wrote to Burke when news of the riots reached Ireland, and Burke quickly reassured him that the Burke family was safe. He told Shackleton he had been advised to leave London but had refused to do so.

> I thought that if my Liberty was now gone, and that I could not walk the streets of this Town with tranquility, I was in no condition to perform the duties for which I ought alone to wish for Life. . . .

We can hardly think of leaving Town. There is much to be done to repair the ruins of families ruined by wickedness masking itself under the colour of religious zeal.

As often happens in disasters, some of the victims were entirely blameless — for example, the babies carried by mothers who looted Langdale's distillery and who were consumed in the flames with their mothers. And the mothers were simply poor, ignorant women, out to get something for nothing. They were not trying to hurt anyone. Even those who behaved violently were not fully responsible for their behavior. They were exploited by those with craftier minds. Those most to blame managed to escape punishment.

When the Lord Mayor of London was called before the Privy Council for questioning, he was reeking of brandy. His refusal to act was the most provocative feature of the riots, but he whined that he couldn't do anything because he had to think of saving his own life. Although he was convicted of neglect of duty, he died before the sentence began.

Lord Gordon was taken to the Tower under a stronger guard than the one that accompanied King Charles I to the scaffold. In February, 1781, he was tried for high treason. But he hired the cleverest and most unscrupulous lawyers available. They won him an acquittal on the grounds of lack of proof that he had had traitorous intentions when he organized his march on Parliament. After he was acquitted, some churches held thanksgiving services to signify approval of the verdict. In 1788 he ran afoul of the law again because he had published a scurrilous book about Marie Antoinette. The French government protested. He was prosecuted and found guilty of libel. But he went into hiding. When he was tracked down, in the Jewish quarter of Birmingham, he was wearing a beard down to his waist. He had become converted to Judaism and had taken the name of Israel ben Abraham. He was then sentenced to prison for five years. But when the time came for his release, nobody could be found who would vouch for his future good behavior. He remained in Newgate Prison, where he died on November 1, 1793, during an epidemic of jail fever.

An oft-repeated story about the riots was the one about the "death" of the Earl of Effingham, whose sympathies with the Americans were so strong that he resigned his commission rather than fight against them. The rumor spread that he had been present at the burning of Newgate Prison and had also led a mob across Blackfriars' Bridge. He was recognized because of the ruffles he wore. But it so happened that he never did wear ruffles. Then his dead body, disguised as a chimney sweep, was found in Fleet Market. The young son of a close friend of Effingham's ran home to tell his father this sad news, only to find Effingham himself standing in his father's drawing room. Effingham soothed the startled boy by saying, "This is my *third* death during the riots." Some time after the riots, Effingham appeared at court wearing a coat that someone admired. Burke observed, "It is the same coat in which he was killed at the riots."

For months following the Gordon Riots wild rumors circulated about their true cause. Such great violence could not be explained by anti-Catholic sentiment alone — there weren't that many people in England who hated Catholics so intensely. The rioters were spurred on by resentments unrelated to religion. The poor of London had had no meaningful outlet for their many frustrations. The rioters, having never known the taste of power, understandably became intoxicated with joy when they found they could get away with beating and humiliating high dignitaries.

Some people thought that the riots were fomented by England's enemies — America, France, Spain. Among the cries of "No Popery!" there were also demands for peace. Instead of blaming the riots on the demented Lord Gordon, some now placed the blame on the pro-American M.P.'s, who were also the supporters of the Catholic Relief Bill. Since the beginning of his public life Burke had been attacked in cartoons, editorials, and pamphlets because of the Catholic influences in his background. Now those attacks were intensified.

The most prolific and perhaps the most vicious of the caricaturists of the late eighteenth century was James Gillray, a man who hated Catholics intensely. Even King George was not immune from Gillray's attacks. Gillray portrayed him as a stupid, bumbling "Farmer George." When the king was quoted as being unable to understand Gillray's caricatures, Gillray got his revenge by drawing a caricature entitled "A Connoisseur Examining a Cooper," which satirized the king's miserly habits and his pretensions to an understanding of art. Gillray's attacks on political figures sometimes bordered on the insane, and he was in fact declared insane near the end of his life. Among the many whom he caricatured savagely, Burke may have been the chief victim.

Burke had become hardened to this sort of thing. He did not let it disturb him unduly. What worried him now was the possibility that the rioters might be punished too severely. If a great many of them were executed, that in itself might provoke another riot. He pointed out that many rioters had already lost their lives during the riots and suggested that only two or three of those who had been arrested should be executed. This suggestion was not followed, but it may have had some effect in reducing the number who were selected for execution. Sixty-two rioters were condemned to death. Only twenty-five were actually executed.

Even though Burke was attacked as the person most responsible for the Gordon Riots, his reputation was high in the summer of 1780. Rumors were circulating that King George, dissatisfied with Lord North, intended to appoint Lord Rockingham as Prime Minister. If that happened, Burke might be appointed to a Cabinet post. But the rumors were without foundation. Lord North would continue as Prime Minister for many months to come.

Yet the Rockingham group had been gaining strength. By this time many independent Members of Parliament had been impressed by Burke. Belatedly, they began to see that his arguments in favor of the Americans had been justified. Now, when he stood up to speak, he could expect more than a few members to listen attentively and to vote for resolutions he supported. On one memorable occasion — April 6, 1780 — the House of Commons went so far as to vote 233-215 in favor of a resolution that the influence of the Crown had increased, was increasing, and should be diminished — this in spite of the fact that the king controlled a large bloc of votes. This resolution was introduced by a Mr. Dunning, one of Burke's supporters. By this time the people of England were showing great dissatisfaction with the way the American war had dragged on. Petitions poured in to Parliament demanding a reform of the electoral system as one way of curbing the power of the king.

On September 3, 1780, the king called for new elections. Burke had to go to Bristol to campaign for reelection, but he knew that he had little chance of winning. Many of his Bristol constituents were angry with him because he had supported the Catholic Relief Act. Some felt that Bristol trade had suffered as a result of recent trade concessions to Ireland. Those who might have wished to support his campaign no longer had the means to do so. The war had ruined their business.

On September 6, 1780, Burke delivered a speech in the Bristol Guildhall in which he defended his entire record as representative from Bristol, with special emphasis on his support of the Catholic Relief Act:

> I was never less sorry for any action of my life . . . . This way of proscribing the citizens by denominations and general descriptions, dignified by the name of reason of state, and security for constitutions and commonwealths, is nothing better at bottom, than the miserable invention of an ungenerous ambition which would fain hold the sacred trust of power, without any of the virtues or any of the energies that give a title

to it; a receipt of policy, made up of a detestable compound of malice, cowardice, and sloth . . . Crimes are the acts of individuals and not of denominations.

But a canvass of the voters showed that he couldn't possibly win. On September 9 he withdrew his candidacy.

Burke's friend Richard Champion, in a letter to Lord Rockingham, described the effect of Burke's speech on the audience:

> I never was present at a more moving Scene. There were, My Lord, very few dry Eyes in Court. When he finished, it was not so much a Plaudit, as a burst of Affectionate Regard. A general Silence succeeded, and we all returned with him to the Town House, with the same degree of Solemnity, as if the people had lost their best friend, and were following him to the grave. The Streets were crowded with people, who though of different parties and of different descriptions, universally joined in the solemn and silent tribute of affectionate Regard.

He would still remain in Parliament, however. Lord Rockingham invited him to represent the pocket borough of Malton in Yorkshire, which was under Rockingham's control. For the rest of his political life Burke would sit in Parliament as representative of that obscure borough.

But whether he represented a large city or a tiny borough, he would remain a dominant figure in Parliament for many years to come. In 1780 he was fifty-one, in the prime of life. Some of his most significant achievements lay in the future.

At about this time another William Pitt was elected to Parliament. The son of the late Earl of Chatham was a tall, thin, rather ungainly youth of twenty-one, but he made his presence felt from the beginning of his politicial career. On February 26, 1781, he delivered his maiden speech when he rose to support Burke's motion to reintroduce his Bill for Economical Reform.

Maiden speeches in the House of Commons were seldom brilliant. Most new members did no more than try their powers in carefully memorized speeches. But everyone wanted to hear from the son of the former Prime Minister. Instead of waiting for him to make a speech on his own initiative, several members called on him to say what he thought of Burke's motion. Speaking extemporaneously, Pitt showed that he had given long and careful thought to the reforms proposed by Burke. He spoke so brilliantly as to leave no doubt that he would do credit to his family name. Burke commented, "He is not a chip of the old block; he is the old block itself." Some members hurried to shake Pitt's hand in congratuluation.

By the spring of 1781 the outcome of the American war was still in doubt. In spite of aid from France and Spain, the Americans were by no means certain of ultimate victory. And King George had no intention of ending the fight until Britain had dragged the Americans back to the British Empire.

Then, in October, 1781, came the battle that is considered the final and decisive battle of the American Revolution (although some fighting went on for months thereafter). On October 17, precisely four years after Burgoyne's surrender at Saratoga, a British drummer stepped up on the parapet of the inner defenses at Yorktown, Virginia, and beat the signal for a parley. The firing ceased. Negotiations for surrender began. Two days later 7,247 British soldiers and 540 British seamen laid down their arms. The great American General George Washington had triumphed over the great British General Cornwallis.

Yet as late as November 3, 1781, King George received dispatches from America indicating that Cornwallis was sure to defeat the Americans. The jubilant king expressed faith in the assistance of Divine Providence.

Not until November 25 did the news of the fall of Yorktown reach London. When Lord North heard the news, he paced up and down in his apartment at 10 Downing Street, moaning repeatedly, "Oh God! It is all over!"

15. And the Treaty of Peace Is Signed
(1782)

KING GEORGE RECEIVED the news of the fall of Yorktown with outward calm. He could not admit that it meant
the end of the war, with England on her knees to America
instead of the other way around. He wrote a note to Lord
Germain, Minister of War:

> I trust that neither Lord Germain nor any member of the
> Cabinet will suppose that it makes the smallest alteration in
> those principles of my conduct which have directed me in past
> time and which will always continue to animate me under
> every event in the prosecution of the present contest.

One detail about this note was odd and signficant. The
king made a practice, when writing notes, of indicating the
precise hour and minute when the note was written. He
failed to include this information in his note to Germain.

But if King George still believed in continuing the American war, he could no longer count on support from Parliament. The opposition members made several motions to
bring the war to a formal close. Loyalty to the king was still
strong enough to prevent those motions from passing. But
the opposition members intensified their attacks. With
each new motion they gained a few more votes.

Meanwhile, news of other disasters followed the news of
the fall of Yorktown. The French captured several islands in

the West Indies. A French squadron was threatening British communications in India. The combined French and Spanish fleets continued to prowl in the English Channel. The Spanish captured Minorca. Crowds gathered in London to demand an end to the war. By the close of February, 1782, nearly all of the M.P.'s except the King's Friends had been won over to the opposition side. There wasn't a ghost of a chance that Lord North's ministry could be saved.

By March 20 the opposition knew that they had a clear majority ready to overthrow that ministry. Most of the members arrived early that afternoon, anticipating a long debate. Several skilled orators, including Burke, were prepared to launch an attack on North. They waited and waited, fiddling around with routine business, until North arrived. He showed up at four-fifteen, in formal dress, with the ribbon of the Order of the Garter across his breast. Immediately, Lord Surrey, who had been chosen to open the debate, signaled the Speaker. At the same instant Lord North also signaled the Speaker. There was an uproar. Some members shouted "Surrey!" Some shouted "North!" Finally North shouted above the din that any action from the opposition was unnecessary. His ministry had ceased to exist. This announcement shocked everyone into silence. North then delivered a gracious resignation speech.

A few members muttered that his administration still needed to be investigated. North answered coolly that he did not plan to run away. He would answer for his conduct. The House adjourned, and the members hurried out to call their carriages. But North, knowing that he would be inside for only a short time, had ordered his carriage to be kept waiting at the head of the line. The other members hurried after him, fuming at having missed a chance to deliver their carefully prepared speeches. As they stood in the drenching rain, Lord North made a courtly bow, stepped into his carriage, and said, "You see, gentlemen, the advantage of being in on the *secret*. Goodnight." His driver cracked the whip, and the carriage sped away.

After North resigned, a feeling of relief swept over the nation. Even Samuel Johnson had by this time become disgusted with the North administration. "Such a bunch of imbecility," he said, "never disgraced a country. If they sent a messenger into the City to take up a printer, the messenger was taken up instead of the printer, and committed by the sitting Alderman. If they sent one army to the relief of another, the first army was defeated and taken before the second arrived. I will not say that what they did was always wrong, but it was always done at a wrong time."

During the dreadful weeks after the fall of Yorktown King George finally learned to accept the unacceptable fact that he had lost America. That loss caused him such agony that he wanted to abdicate and go live in Hanover, home of his German ancestors. But he did not do so. Instead, he came to terms with the opposition and named Lord Rockingham as his new Prime Minister.

It may seem surprising that Rockingham, in selecting his Cabinet, did not appoint Burke to a ministerial post. Some believed it was because of Burke's personal deficiencies — his emotional nature, lack of a distinguished family background, less-than-polished manners. But Rockingham's motives may actually have been generous. Knowing that Burke was hopelessly in debt, Rockingham may for that reason have appointed him to a job that could have been highly lucrative — the job of Paymaster-General of the Forces. The Paymaster-General was allowed to speculate with public funds and to deposit the profits and the interest in his personal account. Men who had held the position previously had enriched themselves beyond the dreams of avarice.

But Burke had been advocating economic reform. Now, instead of taking advantage of his position to enrich himself, he allotted himself a straight salary of 4,000 pounds a year plus the use of a house in Whitehall — a small fraction of what he might have taken without incurring criticism. He also found jobs for his son Richard and for his Bristol friend Richard Champion as deputy paymasters at salaries of 500 pounds a year each. Shortly afterward, more as a tribute to his father than because of his own merits, young Richard Burke was elected a member of the Club at the exceptionally early age of twenty-four. As Paymaster-General Burke was also able to offer benefits to other friends and relatives, including his sister, Mrs. Juliana French, for whom he got a pension of 200 pounds a year. He also got commissions for paintings and sculptures for some of his needy young artist friends.

Burke's generosity to members of his own family and friends in distributing jobs and other benefits may seem ethically questionable. But even in our own day standards of morality may vary greatly from one administration to the next. Compared with those who had previously held the post of Paymaster, Burke was almost niggardly about the benefits he accorded himself. He was actually saving the country some 27,000 pounds annually. And he took none of the benefits of his office with him after retirement, whereas Lord Holland, father of Burke's friend Charles James Fox, managed to pocket nearly 250,000 pounds in interest by holding the balances for thirteen years after he retired as Paymaster.

All new administrations have the task of cleaning up the messes — or what they consider messes — left by the preceding administration. But few new administrations have been faced with a mess as monumental as the one that the Rockinghams had to deal with. They had to take over the reins of power of a nation that had suffered disgrace in the eyes of the world, a disgrace now being gloated over in other European capitals. They had to deal with the stagger-ing economic problems resulting from a costly war, and with a king too proud to admit his responsibility for his country's sufferings. The Rockinghams plunged in to accomplish what they could, and within a few weeks put through several pieces of legislation, including some provisions of Burke's plan for economic reform.

But Burke was concerned with reform in only a limited way. He disliked making changes in an existing situation unless such changes were clearly for the better. And he was cool to reforms initiated by others. He strongly disagreed, for example, with young William Pitt's proposal for changes in the methods by which M.P.'s were elected. Burke did not consider the existing system unsatisfactory. He considered the common man unfit to decide how he should be governed. The idea that representation should be proportional to population made no sense to Burke. The people's "interests" were represented in Parliament. The people themselves did not need to be represented.

In the debate on the electoral reform bill proposed by Pitt, Burke said loftily:

> I look with filial reverence on the constitution of my country and never will cut it into pieces, and put it into a kettle of any magician, in order to boil it, with the puddle of their compounds, into youth and vigour. On the contrary, I will drive away such pretenders. I will nurse its venerable age, and with lenient art extend a parent's breath.

To someone so full of youthful ardor as William Pitt such a statement must have been irritating. It was not calculated to make him feel friendly toward Burke, and they did in fact differ deeply on some issues as the years went by. Burke was fifty-three in 1782, and had served in Parliament for sixteen years. He may well have been a bit condescending toward a youth of twenty-one. Possibly, with the passing years, Burke had become increasingly conservative. Yet even in youth he had shown conservative tendencies. He saw much that was wrong with society. He wished to correct some social evils. But he was wary of change simply for the sake of change or changes that might in the long run do more harm than good.

Today Burke is generally regarded as a conservative statesman, and some of his views are warmly endorsed by today's conservatives. But the person who studies Burke's life with the preconception that he was an arch-conservative will be constantly jolted at evidence that some of his views were quite liberal for his times. It must be kept in mind that he lived in a period when the word "democracy" had different connotations than it has today. The idea of government of the people for the people by the people would have seemed odious to most eighteenth-century politicians. The unwashed mob — as their behavior during the Gordon Riots and other incidents revealed — could be extremely dangerous when invested with power. To Burke, the harm that could be done to a nation by its poor and ignorant citizens was far greater than the harm done by M.P.'s who had been elected by unethical methods. Burke did not live long enough to see the virtues of a democratic system of government after such a system had been in effect for a long time. He was aware only of the possible dangers of destroying a method that, in spite of some defects, worked quite well, and replacing it with a method that corrected those defects only to produce worse defects.

Many examples could be given — and some have already been given — of Burke's liberal tendencies. But one little-known fact about him is that his attitude toward homosexuality was rather liberal for a man of his generation. To suggest that he would have favored "gay rights" would be going too far. But he was horrified at the punishment meted out to those found guilty of homosexuality. When two male homosexuals were sentenced to the pillory, they were stoned by a jeering mob. One of them was killed. Burke made a speech about the incident in the House of Commons and asked for repeal of the law that subjected homosexuals to such inhumane treatment. As a result he was subjected to slanderous gossip and to attacks in the press.

The *Morning Post* defended the behavior of the mob. "Every *man*," the newspaper said, "applauds the spirit of the spectators, and every *woman* thinks their conduct right. It remained only for the patriotic Mr. Burke to insinuate that the crime these men committed should not be held in the highest detestation, and that it deserved a milder chastisement than ignominious death."

Burke managed to get a pension for the widow of the murdered man and also sued the author of the article, William Finney, claiming that Finney had encouraged people to murder homosexuals. Finney was sentenced to three months' imprisonment.

In view of this and other instances of Burke's liberality, we would misjudge him if we assumed that he was complacent about the injustices that existed in his day. True, he was more concerned about some types of injustice than about others. But he did fight for justice on many fronts. More cannot be said of many men.

How much the Rockingham administration might have accomplished had it lasted for an appreciable length of time can only be surmised, for it ended abruptly only three months after it began. Rockingham died on July 1, 1782. His death, which came suddenly, was a great blow to Burke. Burke's friendship with Rockingham had never had the intensity of his friendships with literary and artistic men. Still, he and Rockingham were fond of each other and enjoyed social relations, in addition to their work in Parliament. Rockingham's death meant the end of Burke's job as Paymaster-General. And without Rockingham to back him Burke's power in Parliament was diminished.

When Rockingham's mausoleum was erected, Burke composed the epitaph: "He far exceeded all other Statesmen in the art of drawing together, without the seduction of self-interest, the concurrence and co-operation of the various dispositions and abilities of men whom he assimilated to his character, and associated with his labours."

As Rockingham's successor the king chose Lord Shelburne, a man whom Burke described as having the principles of Machiavelli, the morals of Catiline and Cesare Borgia. The Shelburne ministry lasted only nine months and was notable chiefly for the fact that the peace treaty between the United States of America and England was negotiated during those months. Burke played no official part in those negotiations. His interest in America dwindled once it ceased to be part of the British Empire. But he did care what might happen to the new nation. He was concerned about whether it might long endure. This was partly because he distrusted democratic insitutions. But he also had the surprising foresight to suggest that the southern States might one day secede.

In one of his remarkable prophecies, made in his *Address to the British Colonists in North America*, he said:

> That very liberty, which you so justly prize above all things, originated here; and it may be doubtful whether, without being constantly fed from the original fountain, it can be at all perpetuated or preserved in its native purity and perfection. . .
> We apprehend you are not now, nor for ages are likely to be, capable of that form of constitution in an independent state. Besides, let us suggest to you our apprehensions that your present union (in which we rejoice, and which we wish long to subsist) cannot always subsist without the authority and weight of this great and long-respected body, to equipoise, and to preserve you amongst yourselves in a just and fair equality. It may not even be impossible that a long course of war with the administration of this country may be but a prelude to a series of wars and contentions among yourselves, to end at length (as such scenes have too often ended) in a species of humiliating repose, which nothing but the preceding calamities would reconcile to the dispirited few who survived them.

Not until December 5, 1782, did King George summon up the courage to acknowledge the independence of the United States, in a special speech from the throne attended by Members of Parliament, a few foreign notables, and a cluster of forlorn-looking American Loyalists. The king was visibly agitated at having to make such a humiliating pronouncement. Many of the spectators were distressed at seeing the once-proud monarch attempting to hold on to his last shreds of dignity as he sat, clothed in royal robes, reading his speech from a scroll.

But Burke observed the king without pity. Remembering how indifferent the king had been to the suffering of those who fought the war, Burke could not feel sorry for the misguided man. To Burke's ears the speech exuded hypocrisy and false piety.

The king's voice trembled. When he came to the words "offer to declare them . . . ," he paused for a long moment, unable to utter the words that followed. Then, drawing a deep breath, he went on: ". . . true and independent States, by an article to be inserted in the treaty of peace."

It was not simply a desire to save face that had made the king hold off so long before accepting the independence of the United States. What he feared most was the possibility that the colonies would be unable to remain independent very long. They might soon become satellites of France. Should that happen, Britain might lose Canada and her possessions in the West Indies. France would then dominate North America just as Spain and Portugal were dominating South America. And Britain would lose her trade with North America. Something of that sort might well have happened had the colonies indeed been as weak as the king believed and had French power not been weakened during the years of the French Revolution.

16. Crusade for Justice in India
(1781-1788)

BURKE'S EFFORTS ON behalf of America are, of course, of special interest to Americans. But his crusade on behalf of the Americans was less significant to Burke himself than some other causes that he espoused. While he was fighting for the rights of Americans, he was simultaneously devoting much of his time to the needs of Ireland, and he would continue to be concerned about Ireland for the rest of his life.

The concerns of Ireland were particularly significant during the years of the American Revolution and the years immediately following the fall of Yorktown. On June 14, 1782, Henry Flood said in the Irish House of Commons: "A voice from America shouted to liberty, the echo of it caught your people as it passed along the Atlantic, and they renewed the voice till it reverberated here." (Like Burke, Flood was educated at Trinity College in Dublin. Immediately after entering the Irish Parliament in 1759, he began the creation of an opposition to that corrupt body and the education of public opinion in the country.) In no part of the British Empire were the effects of the American Revolution more far-reaching than in Ireland. The Irish were relegated to an inferior status in the Empire comparable to that of the American colonists. The grievances of the Irish — far more substantial than those of the American colonists — were due to similar causes. The Irish were inevitably sympathetic with the Americans in their fight for freedom and had learned from that fight ways of gaining redress for their own grievances.

It is understandable that Burke would have a special affection for Ireland, land of his birth, and for America, a country that shared language and traditions with England. But he fought no harder for the Irish and the Americans than he did for the people of India, with whom he had little in common other than the fact that they were fellow human beings. In his own opinion, the greatest achievement of his life was his crusade for justice in India. Reviewing his public life in 1794, he said:

> If I were to call for a reward, it would be for the services for which for fourteen years, without interruption, I showed the most industry and had the least success. I mean in the affairs of India. They are those on which I value myself the most; the most for the importance; most for the labor; most for the judgment; most for constancy and perseverance in the pursuit.

His interest in India began long before he entered Parliament. At his first meeting with Samuel Johnson, in 1758, Burke had impressed the older man with his knowledge of India. That interest was sustained over the years. By the time the American war ended, Burke's work in Parliament was almost exclusively related to India. He attacked the problem with an intensity that was at times ferocious. The strain of his work and the frustrations he sometimes faced made him sink into spells of depression. During those years he rarely made new friends. Indeed, his moodiness sometimes caused him to lose old friends. But one friend he met after 1780 is of special interest because she was a gifted writer who left vivid accounts of what he was like when he was in his fifties and sixties.

Fanny Burney was a young novelist whose first novel *Evelina* was published anonymously in 1778, when she was twenty-six. Since it became the talk of the town, she couldn't keep her identity a secret very long. Much to her consternation — for she was shy and ill at ease in fashionable social gatherings — she became a celebrity and was invited to the homes of the bluestockings. For years she had admired Burke and longed to meet him, but she did not enjoy that pleasure until June, 1782, when both of them attended a dinner at the home of Sir Joshua Reynolds. Fanny was seated directly across the table from Burke and thus had an excellent opportunity to observe him and to listen, enraptured, to his conversation. She confided in her diary that she was "quite desperately and outrageously in love" with him and described him thus:

> There was an evident, a striking superiority in his demeanour, his eye, his actions that announced him no common man . . . . He is tall, his figure is noble, his air commanding, his address graceful; his voice is clear, penetrating, sonorous, and powerful, his language is copious, various, and eloquent, his manners are attractive, his conversation is delightful.

Fanny was at that time a spinster of thirty and would remain unmarried until she was forty-one. Although not beautiful, she was attractive in a quiet way. She and Burke were drawn to each other in a way not uncommon between men and women whose intimacy never goes beyond the flirtation stage. Each had a special appreciation for the gifts of the other. Each bloomed in delight at that appreciation. On one occasion, before meeting Burke, Fanny had been invited to dinner at Mrs. Thrale's house and was placed next to Dr. Johnson because of her literary achievements. Her natural shyness was accentuated when she observed Johnson's appalling table manners and listened to his grunts and groans. She sat through the entire meal without uttering a word and felt mortified whenever she recalled that dreadful experience. When Fanny met Burke, she was briefly apprehensive lest she be overcome by an attack of shyness. Instead she found that he didn't make her at all uneasy. He knew her work, had in fact sat up an entire night to read *Evelina*. What he said about it was not polite flattery. It was genuine appreciation. In Burke's presence she sparkled with a wit and intelligence that belied her outwardly demure manner.

After their meeting at Sir Joshua's home Burke and Fanny often saw each other socially, and their faces always lighted up when they met. On one occasion Jane good-naturedly accused them of carrying on a flirtation right under her nose. But Jane had no cause to feel jealous. At no time was Burke romantically linked with any woman but his wife. Jane's relationship with Fanny seems to have been particularly warm. Fanny was fond of Jane and impressed with her "civility and softness of manner." For the rest of Burke's life Fanny would remain his devoted friend and Jane's.

A few weeks after their first meeting — on July 29, 1782 — Burke sent Fanny a letter praising her second novel, *Cecilia*:

Madam,
I should feel exceedingly to blame if I could refuse to myself the natural satisfaction, and to you the just but poor return, of my best thanks for the very great instruction and entertainment I have received from the present you have bestowed on the public. There are few — I believe I may say fairly there are none at all — that will not find themselves better informed concerning human nature, and their stock of observation enriched, by reading your Cecilia. They certainly will, let their experience in life and manners be what it may. The arrogance of age must submit to be taught by youth. You have crowded into a few small volumes an incredible variety of characters, most of them well planned, well supported, and well contrasted with each other. If there be any fault in this respect, it is one in which you are in no great danger of being imitated. Justly as your characters are drawn, perhaps they are too numerous. But I beg pardon; I fear it is quite in vain to preach economy to those who are come young to excessive and sudden opulence.

This criticism may be a bit gushing, but no more so than the kind of letter most persons might write to a friend who has recently published a book. A personal letter doesn't have to meet the same standards as a criticism intended for the reading public. And it is unlikely that Fanny's head was turned by the praise. She had a remarkably keen eye for the nuances of human behavior in others and was quite capable of taking a poke at herself occasionally.

One of the amazing things about her is that she could write so well despite the gaps in her formal education. As the daughter of an organist, she did enjoy the advantages that go with growing up in a family where the other members have been well educated. But she herself didn't even know the alphabet until she was eight years old. Her only formal schooling was a very short period at an English boarding school. Her two sisters were sent to boarding school in Paris while she remained at home, possibly because she was so extremely shy that she would have been miserable if she were sent so far from home. Still, once she learned the alphabet, she must have become a prodigious reader and a compulsive scribbler. While she was in her early teens, she was writing stories and filling pages of a diary. Her ability to reproduce conversations probably surpassed Boswell's. After she published *Evelina,* her life became intertwined with many of the notables of her day: Burke and Reynolds, Johnson and Mrs. Thrale, members of the bluestocking society, King George, Queen Charlotte.

Yet a time came when she felt something close to loathing for Burke, because he was the enemy of another friend of hers, Warren Hastings.

Hastings, born into poverty, was reminded from infancy that his family had once been wealthy and distinguished, but had lost their property during the civil war of the seventeenth century. From boyhood he had longed for the day when he would be rich enough to buy back the land that had once been his family's. Many years would pass before he realized that dream. The price would be far greater than he could ever have imagined.

A wealthy uncle adopted him after his parents died. The uncle sent young Hastings to a fine preparatory school, where the boy made a brilliant record. But the uncle refused to send him on to a university. At the age of sixteen young Hastings had to go to work as a low-salaried clerk with the East India Company in India. For years he worked hard and lived an austere existence while observing other young men coming over from England to work for the East India Company. By robbing the natives and cheating the company, these young men acquired fortunes of several hundred thousand pounds within a few years. Then they returned to England to enjoy their ill-gotten gains. Such men, called "nabobs," were universally despised. Too wealthy and arrogant to return to the social level from which they had sprung, too lacking in social graces to be accepted by the high-born, they belonged nowhere. Yet their wealth brought many advantages. Some married the daughters of peers. Some bought rotten boroughs and thus acquired seats in Parliament for themselves or for persons who would thereafter be in their debt. They bought fine mansions in the better residential areas of London and flaunted their wealth. Other youths, inspired by their example, went off to India to make their own fortunes.

Hastings worked diligently and advanced himself on the strength of his abilities. In 1772, when he was forty, he became governor of Bengal. In 1774 he became the first governor-general of India. During the American war he received few instructions from England and began to develop dictatorial traits. (Power and fame probably meant more to him than wealth.) He frequently got into violent quarrels with his council members. In 1780, as the result of one such quarrel, he fought a duel with Philip Francis, a member of the council. Francis suffered a shoulder wound that would distress him for the rest of his life. Smoldering with resentment, Francis returned to England. Immediately after he reached London, in the fall of 1781, he called on the Burkes, who were old friends of his, presented them with lavish gifts from India, and told them what Hastings had been doing.

Francis was shrewd in selecting Burke as the person to whom to tell this story. Nobody felt so strongly as Burke about cruelty, injustice, oppression of the weak and helpless. Any story about one person using his power to destroy another was sure to arouse Burke's indignation.

Burke now demanded a parliamentary investigation of the administration of the East India Company. That investigation uncovered even greater corruption than Francis had reported. On April 28, 1783, speaking before the House of Commons, Burke pledged himself to God, to his country, to the House of Commons, and to the unfortunate inhabitants of India that he would bring to justice "the greatest delinquent that India ever saw." Following that speech he spent months analyzing all of the documents relating to corruption in India.

On November 18, 1783, Burke's friend Charles Fox introduced a bill in the House of Commons, calling for reforms in India. On December 1, speaking in support of that bill, Burke delivered a three-hour speech in which he claimed that Englishmen were exploiting the Indian people to the ruin of India and the disgrace of the British Empire.

> The Tartar invasion was mischievous; but it is our protection that destroys India. It was their enmity, but it is our friendship. Our conquest there, after twenty years, is as crude as it was the first day. The natives scarcely know what it is to see the gray head of an Englishman. Young men (boys almost) govern there, without society, and without sympathy with the natives. Animated by all the avarice of age and all the impetuosity of youth, they roll in one after another, wave after wave, and there is nothing before the eyes of the natives but an endless, hopeless prospect of new flights of birds of prey and passage, with appetites continually renewing for a food that is continually wasting. Every rupee of profit made by an Englishman is lost forever to India. With us are no retributory superstitions, by which a foundation of charity compensates, through ages, to the poor, for the rapine and injustice of a day. With us no pride erects stately monuments which repair the mischiefs

which pride has produced, and which adorn a country out of its spoils. England has created no churches, no hospitals, no palaces, no schools. England has built no bridges, made no high roads, cut no navigations, dug out no reservoirs. Every other conqueror of every other description has left some monument, either of state or beneficence, behind him. Were we to be driven out of India this day, nothing would remain to tell that it had been possessed, during the inglorious period of our domination, by anything better than the ourangoutang or the tiger.

Fox's bill for reforms in India was carried in the House of Commons by a vote of 217-203. But it failed to pass in the House of Lords, where the East India Company had great influence. Young William Pitt, who had been appointed Prime Minister in 1783, at the age of twenty-four, then drew up another bill proposing reforms in India. It was much milder than Fox's bill, since Pitt made only those proposals that were sure to be accepted. It called for a double form of government in India. The political power exercised by the Court of Directors of the East India Company was subordinated to a Board of Control appointed by the king. The governor-general and the presidents and members of councils were to be appointed and removable by the king. A special court was instituted to try company officers charged with misconduct.

Burke was disgusted with Pitt's bill, since it did so little to correct conditions in India and made no reference to the misconduct of Hastings. Burke was determined that Hastings be brought to justice.

On July 30, 1784, Burke appeared in the House of Commons carrying seventeen volumes of reports made by his investigatory committee. Laying his hand on one of those volumes, he said:

I swear by this book, that the wrongs done to humanity in the eastern world shall be avenged on those who have inflicted them. They will find, when the measure of their iniquity is full, that Providence is not asleep. The wrath of Heaven will sooner or later fall upon a nation, that suffers, with impunity, thus to oppress the weak and innocent. We had already lost one empire, perhaps, as a punishment for the cruelties authorized in another. And men might exert their ingenuity in qualifying facts as they pleased but there was only one standard by which the judge of all the earth would try them. It was not whether the interests of the East India Company had made them necessary, but whether they coincided with the prior interests of humanity, of substantial justice, with those rights which were paramount to all others.

Burke's fight against injustices in India would continue for many years. Before his crusade ended, he would have lost many who had been dear to him. Among them was Samuel Johnson.

In December, 1784, Johnson knew his life was nearing its end. He was now seventy-five, and his health had never been good. Since he had ceased to be friendly with Mrs. Hester Thrale, he no longer lived at her home. He had moved to simpler quarters in Bolt Court. There his friends called on him frequently.

During his final illness Johnson was attended by Dr. Richard Brocklesby, who, like Burke, was an alumnus of Ballitore. Brocklesby had great affection for Johnson and thought so well of Burke that he once presented him with 1,000 pounds and offered to renew the gift "every year until your merit is rewarded as it ought to be at court." During Johnson's final week he quoted to Brocklesby the lines from *Macbeth* beginning:

> Canst thou not minister to a mind diseas'd,
> Pluck from the memory a rooted sorrow,
> Raze out the written troubles of the brain?

To which Brocklesby replied with the reply made by the doctor in *Macbeth:*

> Therein the patient
> Must minister to himself.

Toward the end Johnson refused to take any more medicine, saying he didn't want to meet God in a state of idiocy, or with opium in his head.

One day Fanny Burney and Burke were among the several visitors. Johnson pressed Fanny's hand and said, "Do not linger in coming again for my letting you go now." She turned, with tears in her eyes, to leave the room. He called her back and said, "Remember me in your prayers."

Burke said, "I am afraid, Sir, that such a number of us must be oppressive to you."

"No, Sir," said Johnson, "it is not so. And I must be in a wretched state indeed when your company would not be a delight to me."

Burke's voice broke as he replied, "My dear Sir, you have always been too good to me."

That was Burke's last meeting with Johnson. A few days later, on December 13, Johnson died. Burke was one of the pallbearers at the funeral service, which was held at Westminster Abbey on December 20.

17. The Trial of Warren Hastings
(1788-1795)

WHEN BURKE MOVED for papers of impeachment against Hastings, in the spring of 1786, he faced almost insurmountable obstacles. Some members of the House of Commons saw no reason for impeaching Hastings, since he had resigned as governor-general of India and returned to England in 1785. The impeachment process would be time-consuming, expensive, tedious. It would reveal things about colonial administration that might disgrace England in the eyes of the world. The powerful East India Company would make every effort to avoid having its dirty linen washed in public. Besides, Hastings was a favorite of the king and could count on the support of those whose votes were controlled by the king. Also the support of the nabobs who had bought seats in Parliament.

Then why bother? Why did Burke care so intensely about bringing Hastings to justice that he would carry on the fight even against such heavy odds? Was it vindictiveness? Yes, vindictiveness was one factor. But whatever satisfaction Burke might get out of seeing Hastings properly punished, other elements weighed more heavily. The crimes against India were, in Burke's eyes, so enormous that they had to be made known to the world even if he himself should suffer more than his intended victim.

The impeachment process, simple in theory, is quite complicated in practice, as Americans learned in the summer of 1974, when President Richard Nixon was on the verge of being impeached. So complicated that impeachment is rarely used against high government officials. The process of impeachment, which originated in England during the Middle Ages, was intended as a weapon by which a legislative body might remove an unfit person from office. It provided that a lower house of the legislative body should consider evidence against an official. If the lower house should find that evidence strong enough to warrant a trial, it could vote for impeachment. Impeachment has some similarities with an indictment by a grand jury. It does not indicate that guilt has been proved; it simply means that the evidence against an accused official is strong enough to justify a trial. The trial is then held before the upper house of the legislature, which may vote either to convict or to acquit. If the official is convicted, he is removed from office and must pay the penalties for crimes of which he has been found guilty.

There are some parallels between the case of President Nixon and the case of Hastings. Both men resigned from office before the lower house of the legislature concluded the impeachment process. Therefore, they could not be removed from office if found guilty. But in the case of Hastings the impeachment process was not cut off in an early stage. Even before moving for papers of impeachment against Hastings, Burke had succeeded in exposing corruption in India. But he wanted more than that. The impeachment of Hastings became an obsession with Burke. Probably nobody else would have been willing to assume the monumental task of bringing Hastings to justice. But Burke did have the aid of two remarkable young M.P.'s in presenting charges to the House of Commons: Charles Fox, who had been a staunch supporter of Burke ever since Burke delivered his speech on conciliation with America on March 22, 1775; and Richard Brinsley Sheridan, an Irish playwright.

Charles Fox, descended illegitimately from King Charles II, was elected to Parliament when he was only nineteen. He had been spoiled outrageously as a child and was a reckless gambler and heavy drinker. Yet he was an extraordinarily effective M.P. After he took his seat in the House of Commons in 1768, he spoke frequently — and he spoke with wit, skill, and force.

Fox's figure was grossly heavy, his dark-jowled face was dominated by shaggy eyebrows. His speeches were studded with earthy expressions. He did not look the part of the great English statesman, particularly during the American war, when he persisted in wearing buff and blue, the colors of George Washington's army. Yet his skill at impromptu speech was probably matched by none of his contemporaries. Other M.P.'s might rise to leave the House when Burke embarked on a long speech. They were unlikely to leave while Fox was delivering one of his brief, pungent comments.

Sheridan was the son of an actor Burke had known in Dublin during his student days at Trinity College. Before entering Parliament, Sheridan had made a brilliant record as a playwright. In 1775, when he was still in his early twenties, three of his plays appeared simultaneously on the London stage: *The Rivals, Saint Patrick's Day,* and *The Duenna.* A few years later, his plays *The School for Scandal* and *The Critic* left no doubt of his supreme talent for writing comedies of manners. He entered Parliament in 1780, at the age of twenty-nine, and made a strong impression with his speeches, partly because he was something of an actor and knew how to use words and gestures entertainingly.

Fanny Burney, who met him in 1779, described him thus:

Mr. Sheridan has a very fine figure, and a good though I don't think a handsome face. He is tall, and very upright, and his appearance and address are at once manly and fashionable, without the smallest tincture of foppery or modish graces.

The Burke-Fox-Sheridan team made a matchless trio. Each of them displayed a type of oratory that supplemented the talents of the others. Burke was the most profound. Fox had the greatest talent for presenting arguments lucidly. Sheridan's display of Irish wit delighted his audience.

Without the aid of Fox and Sheridan, Burke might not have been able to convince the House of Commons that Hastings should be impeached. With their aid, he scored the greatest parliamentary victory of his career when the House of Commons, on May 10, 1787, voted to impeach Hastings. On May 14 Burke carried the articles of impeachment to the House of Lords.

The trial, which began in Westminster Hall on February 13, 1788, was the most exciting political event within the memory of living man. Many of those who witnessed the trial left records in letters and diaries, but the most memorable description may have been the one written by Thomas Babington Macaulay, an English historian born twelve years after the trial opened:

> Neither military nor civil pomp was wanting. The avenues were lined with grenadiers. The streets were kept clear by cavalry. The peers, robed in gold and ermine, were marshalled by the heralds under Garter King-at-Arms . . . There was seated round the queen the fair-haired young daughters of the house of Brunswick. There the Ambassadors of great Kings and Commonwealths gazed with admiration on the spectacle which no other country in the world could present. There Siddons, in the prime of her majestic beauty, looked with emotion on a scene surpassing all the imitations of the stage. There the historian of the Roman Empire thought of the days when Cicero pleaded the cause of Sicily against Verres . . . . There were seen, side by side, the greatest painter and the greatest scholar of the age. There were the members of that brilliant society which quoted, criticized, and exchanged repartees under the rich peacock hangings of Mrs. Montagu.

(Mrs. Sarah Siddons, who was thirty-two at the time that the trial began, was considered the greatest tragedienne of her day. She was one of several women who fainted upon hearing of tortures inflicted on Indian women. The "historian of the Roman Empire" was Edward Gibbon. The "greatest painter" was Sir Joshua Reynolds. The "greatest scholar" was Dr. Samuel Johnson, but here Macaulay is in error. Johnson did not live to see the Hastings trial. Mrs. Montagu was the famous bluestocking.)

Westminster Hall, the most magnificent room in the Palace of Westminster, was 240 feet long, 68 feet wide, with a roof carried upon elaborately carved hammer beams. Some of the most famous trials in English history had been held there, including those of Sir Thomas More and King Charles I. In preparation for the Hastings trial it had been outfitted with red-covered seats for all but the members of the House of Commons, whose seats were green. To the left were the peers; to the right, the Commons. Peeresses and ticket holders sat in galleries above these seats.

The demand for tickets at the early sessions of the trial was so great that seats sold for as high as fifty guineas each, and every seat was taken. But the proceedings on the first two days were rather dull. The clerks spent most of the time reading the twenty charges against Hastings. A major allegation was that he had doubled the tribute levied upon Cheyt Singh, Rajah of Benares, thus driving the rajah into rebellion. Hastings then deposed the rajah and exacted the same immense tribute from his successor. Hastings was also accused of confiscating the treasures of the Begum of Oude, then subjecting the captive princesses to great indignities and torturing their servants. In addition, he was charged with violations of treaties, misappropriation of funds, and other corrupt acts.

The real drama began at noon on the third day of the trial. The galleries had been packed since eight o'clock. Since spectators were allowed to eat while they watched, the clatter of knives, forks, and glasses continued even after the trial started. Fanny Burney, who was now the Second Keeper of the Robes for Queen Charlotte, received tickets from the queen for that day and the following two days. She filled forty pages of her diary with a description of what went on during those three days.

Probably no other spectator felt emotions as mixed as hers, for she had long idolized Burke. Yet she had become quite friendly with Hastings after his return from India. She considered Hastings an innocent and noble person, and was appalled that Burke should treat him so meanly. Months before the trial began she wrote in her diary: "Mr. Burke is the name in the world most obnoxious (at Court), both for his Reform Bill, which deeply affected all the household, and for his prosecution of Mr. Hastings."

Now Burke appeared in the guise of a villain.

I shuddered, and drew involuntarily back, when, as the doors were flung open, I saw Mr. Burke, as Head of the Committee, make his solemn entry. He held a scroll in his hand, and walked alone, his brow knit with corroding care and deep labouring thought — a brow how different to that which had proved so alluring to my warmest admiration when first I met him! so highly as he had been my favourite, so captivating as I had found his manners and conversation in our first acquaintance, and so much as I owed to his zeal and kindness to me and my affairs in its progress! How did I grieve to behold him now the cruel Prosecutor (such to me he appeared) of an injured and innocent man!

Following Burke came the other managers of the trial, including Fox and Sheridan. Then the members of the House of Commons marched in and took their seats. (Lady Claremont, who was seated in Fanny's box, looked at them through her opera glasses, referring to them as "all those creatures that filled the green benches, looking so little like gentlemen, and so much like hairdressers.") Then came a procession of clerks, lawyers, peers, bishops, and officers, King George's sons and his grandson. (The king never attended the trial.) The Lord Chancellor wound up the procession.

After everyone was seated, a sergeant-at-arms called loudly: "Warren Hastings, Esquire, come forth! Answer to the charges brought against you; save your bail, or forfeit your recognizance!"

A good ten minutes elapsed before Hastings entered the hall. He looked innocuous. He was only five feet six inches tall and weighed about a hundred and twenty pounds. His face was haggard, almost emaciated. Even his poppy-colored suit looked drab in a hall draped in crimson cloth, with the Members of Parliament wearing court dress, the peers and princes in coronation robes, the galleries packed with people dressed in the most flamboyant of eighteenth-century fashions.

Hastings moved slowly down the aisle, with a bailiff at either side of him. When he reached the bar, he dropped on his knees. The Lord Chancellor gave him leave to rise. Hastings stood and bowed deeply. Then the Crier proclaimed: "Warren Hastings, Esquire, late Governor-General of Bengal, is now on trial for high crimes and misdemeanours, with which he was charged by the Commons of Great Britain. All persons whatsoever who have aught to allege against him are now to stand forth."

The Lord Chancellor then made a brief speech, to which Hastings replied, "I come before your Lordships, equally confident in my own integrity, and to the justice of the Court before which I am to clear it."

In Burke's opening speech, which took up four sessions of the trial, he presented the historical background of India and accused Hastings of crimes of deliberation, proceeding from "a heart dyed deep in blackness . . . a heart corrupted, vitiated, and gangrened to the core." He said that the purpose of the trial was to decide "whether millions of mankind shall be miserable or happy," governed unjustly or justly, and whether Britain would exercise wisely, before God, the trust her position imposed upon her.

Bluestocking Hannah More recorded her reaction to this speech:

I was overpersuaded by Lord and Lady Amherst to go to the trial and heard Burke's famous oration of three hours and a quarter without intermission. Such a splendid and powerful oration I never heard, but it was abusive and vehement beyond all conception. Poor Hastings sitting by, and looking so meek to hear himself called villain and cut-throat, &c! The recapitulation of the dreadful cruelties in India was worked up to the highest pitch of eloquence and passion, so that the orator was seized with a spasm which made him incapable of speaking one more word, and I did not know whether he might not have died in the exertion of his powers, like Chatham. I think I never felt such indignation as when Burke, with Sheridan standing on one side and Fox on the other, said, "Vice incapacitates a man from all public duty; it withers the powers of his understanding, and makes his mind paralytic." I looked at his two neighbors, and saw they were quite free from any symptoms of palsy.

Fanny Burney, still torn between her concern for Hastings and her adoration of Burke, listened to this opening speech with dread. Hastings, it seemed at first, was certain to be convicted. But as the speech went on and on, the intellectual side of her nature dominated over the emotional side. She began to perceive that Burke might be defeating his own purposes by the tactics he was using:

When he came to his two narratives, when he related the particulars of those dreadful murders, he interested, he engaged, he at last overpowered me; I felt my cause lost. I could hardly keep on my seat. My eyes dreaded a single glance towards a man so accused as Mr. Hastings; I wanted to sink on the floor, that they might be saved so painful a sight. I had no hope he could clear himself; not another wish in his favour remained. But when from his narration Mr. Burke proceeded to his own comments and declamation — when the charges of rapacity, cruelty, tyranny, were general, and made with all the violence of personal detestation, and continued and aggravated without any further fact as illustration: then there appeared more of study than of truth, more of invective than of justice; and, in short, so little of proof to so much of passion, that in a very short time I began to lift up my head, my seat was no longer uneasy, my eyes were indifferent which way they looked, or what object caught them; and before I was myself aware of the declension of Mr. Burke's powers over my feelings, I found myself a mere spectator in a public place, and looking all around it, with opera-glass in my hand!

(But if Hastings appeared to be a pitiable figure to some spectators in Westminster Hall, it should be noted that he had time to recover from the strain of those sessions during the long intervals when no sessions were being held. He still had many friends in high places. He was still enjoying a rich social life. He had moved to a mansion on Park Lane, and decorated that mansion with magnificent furnishings shipped from India. Burke was furious at such a display of extravagance by a man who pleaded poverty. During the intervals between sessions Burke himself had to work prodigiously at labors relating to the trial.)

The trial became tedious as the days went by, and attendance dropped off sharply. At the end of fifteen sittings the managers had completed their presentations of only two of the twenty charges. By the end of 1788 only thirty-five sittings had been held. During 1789 there were several interruptions because of critical situations at home and abroad (the serious illness of the king and the outbreak of the French Revolution); only seventeen sittings were held that year. In 1790 only fourteen sittings were held. Hastings did not begin to speak in his own defense until June 2, 1791; only five sittings were held that year. In 1792, twenty-two sittings were held; in 1793, another twenty-two sittings; in 1794, twenty-eight sittings. The trial did not end until 1795 — more than seven years after it began.

In his defense speech Hastings offered to accept the Lords' "immediate judgment" without presenting a defense. Then, without stopping to hear the Lords' answer to this proposal, he went on to defend himself. He claimed that the prosecution managers had not supported their charges with evidence. The prosperity of India refuted the charge that he had ruined the country. Affidavits from Indians, attesting to his character and to their affection for him, refuted the charge that he had oppressed the Indian people. Financial data refuted that of mismanagement.

These arguments could not stand up under cold analysis. The fact that India was still prosperous was no proof that Hastings had not misused funds. The fact that some Indians thought well of him was no proof that he had not mistreated other Indians. Financial data might well show that the East India Company was operating at a profit, yet fail to reveal that those profits had been misused.

The Lords recessed to consider the defense. The trial was not resumed until February 14, 1792, when the defense lawyers took over. They conducted their arguments on May 28, 1793.

By this time everyone was blaming everyone else for the long duration of the trial. Burke had quarreled with old friends. He was being ridiculed in newspapers and caricatures for his overemotional behavior during the trial.

Had it not been for that trial, he would have retired from Parliament shortly after he passed his sixtieth birthday. He wanted desperately to put his parliamentary career behind him. But he kept postponing the retirement year after year so that he could bring Hastings to justice.

On May 28, 1794, he began to sum up before the House of Lords his work of fourteen years on behalf of India. The speech, which went on for nine sittings of the trial, ended on June 16, 1794. A speech lasting that long is unlikely to sustain interest. Burke's speech was particularly boring because most of it simply repeated things that he had already said many times during the trial. No doubt the Lords felt relieved when he came to his final sentence: "May you stand a sacred temple, for the perpetual residence of an inviolable justice."

On June 20, 1794, Pitt moved the thanks of the House of Commons to the managers of the trial. He defended them against accusations that they had delayed the trial and claimed that the trial had not been inordinately long, considering its importance. The tone of the speech indicated that Pitt believed that Hastings had deserved impeachment. But in the debate that followed this speech, opponents of the motion hurled abuse at Burke. Fox and Sheridan, temporarily forgetting their differences with Burke over the French Revolution, sprang to his defense. Pitt's motion was finally carried 50-21.

Now Burke rose to speak. It would be his last appearance in the House. He expressed the managers' gratitude for the thanks of the House and deported himself with quiet dignity.

Burke was not present on April 29, 1795, the day when the House of Lords announced its verdict. By heavy majorities, Hastings was acquitted on every count. But the cost of defending himself had left him heavily in debt. The East India Company gave him enough money to buy back the lands that had once belonged to his family, and he went there to live in retirement.

The day on which the verdict was announced, the most suspenseful of the trial, the audience was the largest of the entire proceedings. When the peers had finished pronouncing their judgments on each charge, the Lord Chancellor said to Hastings, who was standing at the bar, "You are acquitted of the articles of impeachment. . .and you are discharged, paying your fees." There was a slight burst of applause from the galleries. Hastings bowed and withdrew. And the peers adjourned to their chamber.

Burke had long expected an acquittal. Yet he was disappointed at the verdict. It made him feel that he had little to show for fourteen years of exhausting labor. Yet the Hastings trial did accomplish something in revealing the evils of colonialism. And Lord Cornwallis, when he was appointed governor-general of India in 1786, accepted that post only with the understanding that he would be allowed to introduce certain reforms. Possibly he would have wanted reform even if Burke had not by that time started to expose the Hastings administration. But it is to be hoped that Cornwallis and others would never repeat the Hastings errors. Furthermore, Burke's speeches, for generations to come, would be studied by English schoolboys destined to serve as colonial officers or Members of Parliament. There is no way of estimating how great Burke's influence may have been on Britain's later colonial policies, not only in India, but in the many other lands that once constituted the great British Empire.

Cornwallis did not suffer permanent disgrace after his surrender to Washington at Yorktown. Indeed, he was given a hero's welcome when he returned to England after the American war. It was only fitting that he should be treated so, for he was a fine general and was actually a good friend of the Americans before the outbreak of the war. As a member of the House of Lords during the years leading up to the war, he was one of the few who opposed the taxes levied on America.

Burke's concern about the plight of India is all to his credit. Less to his credit is his complete lack of compassion for Hastings, although he must have perceived how the accused man was suffering as the trial dragged on and on. Burke was severely — and justifiably — criticized for the intemperate language he used during the trial. He described Hastings as "a rat," "a weasel," "a keeper of a pig sty, wallowing in corruption," "a swindling Maecenas," "a bad scribbler of absurd papers." At times during the trial Burke's language was so violent that Hastings cried out in protest. After the trial was over Burke was charged with having wasted an enormous amount of time and money in attacking a man who was eventually acquitted. But how can one assess how much time and money should be spent in the cause of justice?

The feeling that Hastings had "suffered enough" may have been a major reason for his acquittal. But it must be remembered that the vote for acquittal was not unanimous.

A minority of the lords who voted on the charges did consider Hastings guilty after weighing all the evidence. Even those who voted for acquittal probably did not consider him blameless. Their verdict was undoubtedly influenced by compassion for a man they had seen writhing under the lash of Burke's tongue. Those who voted for acquittal were also swayed by the fact that Hastings, in spite of his misdeeds, had saved the British Empire in India. Everything considered, the lords may have handled the situation as well as possible. Of the one hundred and sixty peers who attended the opening of the trial only twenty-nine were eligible to vote at the end of the trial, since it had been agreed that only those who had attended the session continuously should be allowed to give a verdict. Sixty peers died while the trial was in progress. Others, for one reason or another, were unable to attend year after year after year.

The Hastings case aroused great interest in the United States, where the Constitutional Convention was being held in Philadelphia. Burke had accused Hastings with, among other crimes, waging aggressive war without authority and surrounding himself with a corrupt administration. But it was still disputable whether these constituted valid reasons for impeachment. George Mason, delegate from Virginia to the Constitutional Convention, argued against limiting impeachable crimes to treason and bribery. "Treason," said Mason, "as defined in the Constitution will not reach many great and dangerous offenses. Hastings is not guilty of treason. Attempts to subvert the Constitution may not be treason." Mason suggested adding the phrase "high crimes and misdemeanors" to treason and bribery as grounds for impeachment. And this was done.

Four words with a potency that could have been perceived only dimly by the Founding Fathers!

18. Revolution in France, Discord in England
(1789)

ONLY A FEW MONTHS after the opening of the Hastings trial — in November, 1788 — the royal physicians declared King George III insane and began a course of treatment that might well have driven him insane had he not been mentally deranged in the first place. One physician, Dr. Francis Willis, considered madness a sign of sin, to be dealt with punitively. He strapped the king in his bed and made him sit in a chair equipped with restraining devices. Sometimes Willis used a straitjacket punitively. The other physicians objected to such methods, but their own remedies were no less painful — strong purgatives and blistering mustard plasters. When the king tried to rip off the agonizing plasters, he was punished by being thrust into a straitjacket.

Among the records describing the king's behavior at that time there is probably none more likely to make the reader sympathize with the king than the report in Fanny Burney's diary. As she was living under the same roof as the royal family at that time, as Second Keeper of the Robes for Queen Charlotte, she had firsthand knowledge of the effects of the king's illness on the queen and the young princesses. Fanny's account of the goings-on at Windsor Castle fill so many pages of her diary that it would make a book in itself, a book that gives the reader a "You Are

There" sensation. We see the king as a flesh-and-blood suffering human being, hear the intonations of his pleading voice, feel an impulse to reach across the gulf of time to let him know that we now understand much that was unknown to his contemporaries. The king whose monuments in America were melted down to be shaped into bullets becomes a man who, even while ill and helpless, retains a touching trace of kingliness.

Yet, for all that Fanny received daily bulletins on the state of his health, she couldn't have witnessed the cruelties inflicted on him. She had occasion to speak with the older Dr. Willis several times and, in an entry dated January 3, 1789, described him thus:

> I have made acquaintance with Dr. Willis and his son, and they have desired me to summon one of them constantly for my information.
>
> I am extremely struck with both these physicians. Dr. Willis is a man of ten thousand; open, honest, dauntless, light-hearted, innocent, and high-minded: I see him impressed with the most animated reverence and affection for his royal patient; but it is wholly for his character — not a whit for his rank.
>
> Dr. John, his eldest son, is extremely handsome, and inherits, in a milder degree, all the qualities of his father; but, living more in the general world, and having his fame and fortune still to settle, he has not yet acquired the same courage, nor is he, by nature, quite so sanguine in his opinions.

Fanny's inability to perceive the the uglier traits in the Willises — their pompous self-righteousness, their sadism and opportunism — is understandable when we consider how eager they may have been to make a favorable impression on a woman who might use her skill with words to expose them as pious frauds. She was taken in by them. Yet a little flash of her ability to penetrate beneath the surface does come through in her comment about the younger Dr. Willis "with his fame and fortune still to settle."

The king obviously didn't share Fanny's views. During one of his lucid intervals he rebuked the elder Dr. Willis, who had originally been a clergyman, for turning to the profession of medicine. "You have quitted a profession I have always loved," said the king, "and you have embraced one I most heartily detest." Willis replied that Jesus had cured demoniacs. "Yes," agreed the king, "but he did not get seven hundred a year for it."

During another lucid interval the king revealed his awareness that he had been talking too much. He admitted, "I am getting into Mr. Burke's eloquence, saying too much on little things."

A detailed reproduction of Fanny Burney's report of one encounter with the king, after the worst of his illness was over, may be justified here for what it tells of a side of King George's personality that is unlikely to be mentioned in textbooks intended for American schoolchildren. The incident occurred at Kew Palace on Monday, February 2, 1789.

What an adventure had I this morning! one that has occasioned me the severest personal terror I ever experienced in my life. Sir Lucas Pepys persisting that exercise and air were absolutely necessary to save me from illness, I have continued my walks, varying my gardens from Richmond to Kew, according to the accounts I received of the movements of the King. For this I had her Majesty's permission. . .Taking, therefore, the time I had most at command, I strolled into the gardens. I had proceeded, in my quick way, nearly half the round, when I suddenly perceived, through some trees, two or three figures. Relying on the instructions of Dr. John, I concluded them to be workmen and gardeners; yet tried to look sharp, and in so doing, as they were less shaded, I thought I saw the person of his Majesty!

Alarmed past all possible expression, I waited not to know more, but turning back, ran off with all my might. But what was my terror to hear myself pursued! — to hear the voice of the King himself loudly and hoarsely calling after me: "Miss Burney! Miss Burney!"

I protest I was ready to die. I knew not in what state he might be at the time; I only knew the orders to keep out of his way were universal; that the Queen would highly disapprove of any unauthorized meeting, and that the very action of my running away might deeply, in his present irritable state, offend him. Nevertheless, on I ran, too terrified to stop, and in search of some short passage, for the garden is full of little labyrinths, by which I might escape.

The steps still pursued me, and still the poor hoarse and altered voice rang in my ears — more and more footsteps resounded frightfully behind me — the attendants all running, to catch their eager master, and voices of the two Dr. Willises loudly exhorting him not to heat himself so unmercifully. . . .

When they were within a few yards of me, the King called out: "Why do you run away?"

Shocked at a question impossible to answer, yet a little assured by the mild tone of his voice, I instantly forced myself forward, to meet him, though the internal sensation, which satisfied me this was a step the most proper to appease his suspicions and displeasure, was so violently combated by the tremor of my nerves, that I fairly think I may reckon it the greatest effort of personal courage I have ever made.

The effort answered; I looked up, and met all his wonted benignity of countenance, though something still of wildness in his eyes. Think, however, of my surprise, to feel him put his hands round my shoulders, and then kiss my cheek!

Far from feeling pity for the king, some members of his family and some M.P.'s actually gloated over his misfortune and tried to advance their own interests at his expense. Believing that his father would never recover his reason, the Prince of Wales seized his papers and jewels and tried to take over the functions of a monarch. Fox and Sheridan, close friends of the young prince, were eager to have him appointed regent, with virtually unlimited powers. Acting on their advice, the prince made plans for a complete turnover in the Cabinet. Burke was elated at the prospect. It meant that he would be reappointed Paymaster-General, with all the privileges that he had once enjoyed.

But Pitt, knowing that he would be replaced as Prime Minister if the Prince of Wales seized the reins of power, drew up a Regency Bill that would grant the prince only limited powers. Pitt argued that the prince should not be allowed to do anything the king could not quickly undo after he recovered.

Yet could the king be expected to recover? Did anyone recover from an attack of madness after the age of fifty? Burke tried to make himself an instant expert on mental illness by visiting mental institutions. It wasn't hard for him to get the kind of evidence he wanted. The authorities whom he consulted gave him the statistics he needed for his purpose. Recovery from an attack of madness after the age of fifty was almost unheard of — which is not surprising considering the methods used to cure madness. King George, born on June 4, 1738, was fifty years old in 1788. Therefore, Burke reasoned, he would not recover.

Burke accomplished nothing with this research other than to expose himself to fresh attacks in the press. The *London Times* sarcastically suggested that he had gone to a lot of unnecessary trouble in doing research on a subject with which he was "intimately acquainted," implying that he himself was so unstable that he could have limited his research to a study of his own behavior. As if that weren't enough, King George recovered while the Regency Bill was still in the committee stage. The nation rejoiced. The king would remain in good health until 1801, when he would suffer another, more severe attack of madness. (Not until the 1930's was it realized that he had actually suffered from porphyria, a rare hereditary disease that sometimes causes delirium.)

Burke's speeches relating to the king's illness were at times tasteless. After reading countless case histories of lunatics, he proceeded to recite the details of those cases in the House of Commons until his disgusted audience shouted him down. Once, after Pitt argued that the king, though mad, was still indisputably on the throne, Burke shouted that Pitt was "making mockery of the king, putting a crown of thorns on his head, and a reed in his hand, and dressing him in the purple to cry, 'Hail, King of the British.'"

Burke's behavior during the king's illness was greatly to his discredit. It nearly ruined his political career. Ever since he entered politics he had been abused in cartoons and newspapers. Now that abuse was mixed with derisive pity for a defeated old man. His friends in Parliament had at least temporarily lost status because of their intrigues against the king. Burke's parliamentary career might have ended at that time had he not been so determined to go on with his work on the Hastings trial. In 1789 he could not foresee, of course, that that trial would continue until 1795. Had he been aware of that, he might have been willing to turn over to his younger colleagues the monumental task of prosecuting Hastings. Instead, he remained in Parliament for five more years. During that time he would chalk up a few achievements far more creditable than his behavior during the regency crisis.

Long before Burke entered Parliament he was appalled at what he had learned about the conditions on slave ships and the means by which slaves were captured in Africa. He might have made slavery his major crusade had he not entered Parliament at a time when trouble was brewing in the American colonies. When the American war was nearing its end, he did start to do something about abolishing the slave trade. But then he was diverted by reports of corruption in India. He had to leave to others the task of carrying on an effective fight against the evils of slavery. In 1780 he drafted a paper entitled "Sketch of a Negro Code," in which he suggested rules to cover the slave trade in West Africa, the ships engaged in that trade, the treatment of slaves in passage, the management of slaves in the West Indies. His code provided for education, instruction in "religion and morality," encouragement of family life among slaves. He did not propose emancipation. Few of those who were concerned about slavery at that time believed that emancipation would be a good thing for the slaves, since they might suffer if they were suddenly set free.

The slave trade declined during the American war, when the southern colonies were no longer importing slaves. But it started to boom after the war ended, and the anti-slavery movement grew stronger at the same time. A leader in the movement was William Wilberforce, a graduate of Cambridge University, who took his seat in the House of Commons in 1780, at the age of twenty-one.

On May 12, 1789, Wilberforce introduced twelve resolutions, which, if passed, would result in discontinuing the further importation of slaves to the British West Indies. When Wilberforce concluded his speech, Burke said that it "was perhaps not excelled by anything in Demosthenes." Burke, Pitt, and Fox then delivered speeches supporting Wilberforce's resolutions. But their arguments were countered by the argument that other nations might reap rich profits from the slave trade if England should abolish it. Wilberforce tried to argue that other nations would follow England's example, but that argument was unconvincing. He would have to fight for many years before he succeeded, in 1807, in bringing about abolition of the slave trade. Even then his crusading may have had less effect than the fact that abolition by that time no longer posed a threat to British wealth. Attendance was low in the House of Commons during the abolition debate, and Wilberforce met with little opposition.

He then continued to fight for the emancipation of slaves. The Emancihation Bill, completely abolishing slavery in the British Empire, was not passed until a month after his death in 1833.

Burke was far ahead of his times in asking for revision of the criminal law. He thought — with justification — that the present law failed to distinguish between great and trivial offenses. Thousands who were guilty of minor offenses had suffered such punishment as death on the gallows or transportation to the American colonies. When Samuel Johnson called the Americans "a race of convicts," he was referring to the fact that many of the colonists had been transported to America as convicts. But Johnson, than whom hardly any man ever lived who was more compassionate to the poor, was well aware that many of those convicts had committed crimes no greater than the theft of a few shillings.

After the beginning of the war with the colonies, America could no longer be used as a dumping ground for convicts. Some new place had to be found to which they could be transported. The British West Indies could accommodate only a small proportion of those who now inhabited the pestilence-ridden British jails. In 1785 there was discussion in the House of Commons about the establishment of a penal colony in West Africa or in Australia or New Zealand. During those discussions Burke delivered impassioned speeches about the barbarities of the penal transportation system, claiming that they violated "every principal of justice and humanity." When word of his speech reached Newgate Prison, one prisoner sent him a letter confirming his description of the horrors of transportation.

During the debate on the possible establishment of a penal colony in West Africa, Burke protested that a sentence of transportation to that destination was equivalent to a sentence of death because of the danger of pestilence. Pitt sarcastically accused Burke of having done insufficient research, and tried to brush aside Burke's argument that it was not only the destination against which he was protesting but the entire system of transportation. On July 28, 1785, when Pitt presented a recommendation to establish a penal colony on the Gold Coast, Burke's violent protest may have been a major reason why that project was abandoned. But Burke was practical enough to realize that he couldn't hope to abolish transportation. He supported Botany Bay as an alternative to West Africa. In January, 1788, the first convicts were landed on Australian soil.

Shortly before King George became ill Burke met a man named Thomas Paine, who had been an enthusiastic supporter of the rebel cause in America. Paine, born to a poor family in England in 1737, had enjoyed only a limited formal education. But, by self-education, he had acquired some remarkable skills, including a dazzling skill with words. After he emigrated to America in 1774, he used his writing skill to help the colonists. His pamphlet *Common Sense*, published in January, 1776, was enormously influential in helping to unite the delegates to the Continental Congress on the question of declaring independence from England. "Now is the seed-time of continental union, faith and power," Paine warned. If the colonies dallied in their decision to unite, they might later find it difficult or impossible to form a union.

For several months Paine served with the Continental army, sharing its hardships. Feeling that the ill-equipped troops needed to be convinced of the worth of their cause, he started to publish a series of pamphlets entitled *The Crisis*. The first pamphlet in the series included the majestic words: "These are the times that try men's souls. The summer soldier and the sunshine patriot will, in this crisis, shrink from the service of their country; but he that stands it *now* deserves the love of man and woman." George Washington was so impressed with this pamphlet that he gave orders to have it read to "every corporal guard's army."

Paine knew, of course, of Burke's sympathy with the rebels. When Paine returned to England in 1787, he went to see Burke, and Burke received him cordially. Paine was at that time trying to get financial support for an iron bridge he had designed. Burke helped in this project by taking him on a tour of iron foundries in the Midlands and introducing him to men who might be interested in the bridge. Later Paine spent a week at Beaconsfield. Burke also introduced Paine to several pro-American M.P.'s.

Paine must have been bedazzled at the kind of attention he was getting in England. When he left that country in 1774, he was a nobody, a man of unpolished manners and unprepossessing appearance. Even though he had acquired fame during the intervening years and had won the friendship of a man as distinguished as George Washington, his manners were still crude. Indeed, on one visit to France in 1779 he was so obviously in need of a bath that his host, Ethanah Watson of Philadelphia, urged him to wash up before addressing a group of distinguished French citizens. According to Watson, Paine "was absolutely offensive and perfumed the whole apartment." At Watson's insistence, Paine finally agreed to soak in a tub, but only after he had received a file of English papers to study as he soaked. Watson said of him: "He was coarse and uncouth in his manners, loathsome in his appearance, and a disgusting egotist, rejoicing most in talking of himself, and reading the effusions of his own mind."

Possibly Paine took baths a little more frequently while he was visiting Burke and other prominent Whigs. And they may have met that supreme test of the gentleman — the ability to overlook the lack of gentlemanliness in others. They didn't invite him to their homes simply because of his charm. He brought them valuable information from Thomas Jefferson, Minister to France, and could be forgiven for that reason. But Paine may have been conceited enough to believe that they esteemed him for his personal qualities. At any rate, when he left for France in 1789, he felt he had formed a firm friendship with Burke.

But that friendship was disrupted by the French Revolution, which broke out shortly after Paine arrived in France. Paine, overjoyed that the French people had rebelled against royal tyranny, assumed that Burke, too, would be pleased with what was going on in France. But when Paine suggested to Burke that the Whigs should promote a similar revolution in England, Burke was outraged: "Do you mean to propose that I, who have all my life fought for the British constitution, should devote the wretched remains of my days to conspire in its destruction?"

Paine didn't really understand Burke. For all that Burke was concerned about the rights of oppressed peoples, he

did not believe that the people should overthrow an existing government. Burke was in fact alarmed over the events
in France. The National Assembly — a one-house legislature in which all the people of France were represented —
had swept away all the old institutions of Church and State,
and confiscated Church property. It had transferred property right from one social class to another. Instead of draft-
ing a workable constitution, it had wasted time with pompous declarations about the rights of man. Burke rejected the
"rights of man" demanded by the National Assembly, because that demand was inspired by an irrational desire to be
free of all obligations toward the past and toward posterity.
That demand, if not impeded, could actually subject France
either to anarchy or to the rule of a dictator. In the name of
liberty the French people would overthrow every ancient
freedom. In the name of fraternity they would commit
every atrocity.

When Burke made it clear to Paine that he did not approve of the achievements of the National Assembly, Paine
was stunned. He now assumed that Burke had been hypocritical in setting himself up as the champion of the oppressed. The truth — as Paine perceived it — was that Burke
wasn't sincerely concerned about the rights of the common
people. He believed in an hereditary monarchy and an
hereditary nobility, institutions Paine despised.

Burke spoke often on the subject of an hereditary nobility, but his attitude is perhaps best summed up in a statement made in 1781:

> I am accused, I am told abroad, of being a man of aristocratic
> principles. If by aristocracy they mean the Peers, I have no
> vulgar admiration, nor any vulgar antipathy, towards them. I
> hold their order in cold and decent respect. I hold them to be of
> an absolute necessity in the constitution, but I think they are
> only good when kept within their proper bounds. I trust,
> whenever there has been a dispute between these Houses, the
> part I have taken has not been equivocal. If by the aristocracy,
> which indeed comes nearer to the point, they mean an adher-

ence to the rich and powerful against the poor and weak, this would indeed be a very extraordinary part. I have incurred the odium of gentlemen in the House for not paying sufficient regard to men of ample property. . . .

I would set my face against any act of pride and power countenanced by the highest that are in it; and if it should come to the last extremity, and to a contest of blood — God forbid! God forbid! — my part is taken; I would take my fate with the poor, and low, and feeble. But if these people came to turn their liberty into a cloak for maliciousness, and to seek a privilege of exemption, not from power, but from the rules of morality and virtuous discipline, then I would join my hand to make them feel the force which a few, united in a good cause, have over a multitude of the profligate and ferocious.

Actually Burke had never approved of revolutionary tactics as a means of bringing about social improvement, not even during the American Revolution. He did not regard that war as a revolution anyway; he considered it a civil war. The Americans had not tried to destroy the British system of government. They had simply fought for the rights to which all British subjects had long been entitled.

Many people in England shared Paine's enthusiasm for the French Revolution. Charles Fox voiced the opinion of many other bright young liberals when he said of the fall of the Bastille, "How much the greatest event it is in the world! And how much the best!" Even those in England who did not approve of the actions of the National Assembly regarded the events in France rather smugly. Internal dissension in France would weaken that nation and thus strengthen England's position. Burke was infuriated at the shortsightedness of this attitude. Now he started to make himself obnoxious everywhere he went, disrupting social gatherings with passionate outbursts against the evils of the French Revolution and quarreling with those who disagreed with him.

Younger M.P.'s, who had never known Burke during his early years in the House of Commons, must have formed quite a different opinion of his oratorical style than those who had admired his speeches on behalf of the Americans. One such member was Nathaniel William Wraxall, who was born in 1751 and who entered Parliament in 1780. Wraxall's opinion of Burke was probably shared by most of his contemporaries:

> Throughout his general manner and deportment in Parliament, there was something petulant, impatient, and at times almost intractable, which greatly obscured the lustre of his talents. His very features, and the undulating motions of his head, were eloquently expressive of this irritability, which on some occasions seemed to approach towards alienation of mind. Even his friends could not always induce him to listen to reason and remonstrance, though they sometimes held him down in his seat, by the skirts of his coat, in order to prevent the ebullitions of his anger or indignation. Gentle, mild, and amenable to argument in private society, of which he formed the delight and the ornament, he was often intemperate, and even violent in Parliament.

In the same month that he received Paine's letter about the French Revolution, Burke was distressed by a more personal matter — the death of his sister Juliana. It had been twenty-four years since their last meeting. Even in earlier years he had often gone for long intervals without seeing her. Yet he had always been devoted to her. She seems to have shared his concern for the unfortunate. A story is told of her that she made a practice, every Christmas Day, of inviting to her home the maimed, the aged, the distressed, for a bountiful repast, and waited on them as a servant. When one of her neighbors wrote to tell him of her death, Burke replied, saying: "I was in some hope at times, that I might make the latter part of a life spent under difficulties and afflictions, a little pleasant to her — but that hope, which I believe was hers and my consolation, is vanished and this is one of the greatest and most mortifying disappointments I have felt through life."

In the letter he enclosed a bank draft to provide for the immediate needs of his sister's daughter. Later the daughter came to live at Beaconsfield. Fanny Burney, who met the daughter a few years later, described her as "quite a wild Irish girl," but added that quiet Mrs. Burke would probably "soon subdue this exuberance of loquacity."

On February 9, 1789, in a debate in the House of Commons, Burke expressed his views on the French Revolution in public for the first time. The subject under debate was army estimates. Charles Fox argued for a reduction in army estimates, claiming that France was not a present danger. Burke agreed with Fox on that point, but said he was alarmed lest the English people might be aroused to violence by the example set by France. He went so far as to say he would abandon his best friends and join his worst enemies to resist the contagion from France.

Fox denied any great affection for the French Revolution. What he admired about the events in France, he said, was the spirit of a people fighting for their freedom. He hoped the results of the revolution would be a blessing for both France and England. Burke responded appreciatively to these comments. But at this point Richard Brinsley Sheridan plunged into the debate, made insulting comments about Burke, and enthusiastically defended the French Revolution. Burke was deeply wounded. Sheridan later regretted his hasty words, but Burke no longer regarded him as a friend.

Shortly after their debate Burke decided he would have to write a book warning his countrymen of the dangers England faced if the English people should be infected by ideas emanating from France. The kind of talk he had been hearing from Fox and Sheridan sickened him. Yet it might be influencing others. He would have to answer their arguments in a way that was not possible in parliamentary debate. He placed advertisements in newspapers announcing that he would publish a book about the French Revolution later that year.

19. Reflections on the Revolution in France
(1790)

WHEN PAINE LEARNED that Burke intended to write a book about the French Revolution, he decided to answer that book with a book of his own. Burke's book, Paine knew, would express ideas that Paine found abominable. And Burke's book would probably be highly influential. To counteract that influence Paine felt he must write a book that would show the fallacies in Burke's arguments, a book that would tell what Paine considered the truth about the French Revolution. Paine, after all, had been living in France while the revolution was going on. He saw it happen. As for writing ability, Paine could match his with Burke's. The kind of writing skill that Paine possessed — and that Burke lacked — was a skill in using simple words with sledgehammer force. And Paine had firsthand knowledge of the reading audience to which he would direct his book — the semiliterate working men of England. Like them, he had known what it meant to be desperately poor. He had spent the first thirty-seven years of his life in England. During those years he had done the kind of work available to those born in poverty. He knew how the poor lived. He knew how they thought. He knew their hopes and aspirations and their bitterness at having those aspirations constantly thwarted.

Paine was so eager to start writing his book that he couldn't wait until Burke's book came off the press before putting words on paper. In April, 1790, Paine called on the London bookseller who was going to publish Burke's book and quizzed him about the contents of the book. The bookseller reported that Burke was having trouble with the book. He had rewritten some printed pages as many as nine times. Paine smiled grimly. Evidently Burke was having trouble because he didn't understand what the French Revolution was all about. He couldn't appreciate what it meant to the people of France. Paine started to work on his own book, determined to get it published as soon as possible after Burke's book came off the press.

Burke's *Reflections on the Revolution in France* was published on November 1, 1790. He warned that England, geographically so close to France, could not expect to remain untouched by the "distemper" raging on the other side of the Channel. Should the downtrodden masses of England follow the example of the French, they too might confiscate property in the name of democracy, they too might replace religion with atheism. He was not impressed by the fact that the National Assembly claimed to represent all the people. "A government of 500 country attorneys and obscure curates," he said, "is not good for 24 millions of men though it was chosen by eight and fifty million, nor is it the better for being guided by a dozen of persons of quality who have betrayed their trust in order to obtain that power."

Burke believed that a man has a right to his property, his inheritance, the fruits of his industry, and a fair portion of all that society, with all its combination of skill and force can do in his favor. "Men have equal rights in these matters — but not to an equal share of power, authority, and direction in the management of the state, but to equal opportunity in proportion to their abilities and their social contributions." He claimed that the "right" of men to participate in government was not a natural right of all.

He did not object to changes in government. Indeed, he believed that change is always necessary. "A state without the means of some change is without the means of its own conservation." But when changes are made, they should be changes in which the positive features of the old order are retained.

Thousands of readers, after studying Burke's *Reflections*, began to understand why the French Revolution constituted a menace to England. King George was wildly enthusiastic over the book. "Read it," he would say to everyone who came to see him. "It will do you good — do you good! Every gentleman should read it."

King George began to collect books even before he ascended to the throne, with the thought that his collection would one day form the nucleus of a national library. Among the books that he included in his huge collection were those of many contemporary writers. Almost every first edition of Boswell's books became part of the library. Everything written by Samuel Johnson was purchased immediately after publication. But not until Burke published the *Reflections* did the king begin to assemble a selection of Burke's writings.

Louis XVI liked the book so much that he set himself the task of translating it into French — a task that might better have been entrusted to others, considering what was going on in his country at that time.

Shortly after the *Reflections* was published, more than eighty books and pamphlets were published to rebut its arguments. One of the first — and one of particular interest today, since it was written by a woman with advanced feminist views — was a pamphlet entitled *A Vindication of the Rights of Man*. Its author was Mary Wollstonecraft, the brilliant, self-educated daughter of an Irish ne'er-do-well. In 1792 she would publish a book entitled *A Vindication of the Rights of Woman*, now regarded as the Bible of the feminist movement. She wrote this book after discovering that the French Revolution, despite its goal of creating a society in which all *men* would be free and equal, had little concern for improving the lot of *women*. (She also has some claim to fame as the mother of Mary Wollstonecraft Shelley, author of *Frankenstein*.)

A Vindication of the Rights of Man is, for the most part, a personal attack on Burke, poorly researched and haphazardly organized. Miss Wollstonecraft was pressured to turn out that pamphlet in a hurry by a publisher eager to cash in on a timely subject. Ignoring Burke's earlier speeches, Miss Wollstonecraft concentrated on the speeches he had delivered during the king's serious illness, perhaps the most tasteless speeches that Burke ever delivered. With the outrage of a woman who had experienced oppression and poverty she hurled at Burke the accusation:

> Misery, to reach your heart, I perceive, must have its cap and bells; your tears are reserved, very *naturally* considering your character, for the declamations of the theatre, or for the downfall of queens, whose rank alters the nature of folly, and throws a graceful veil over vices that degrade humanity; whilst the distress of many industrious mothers, whose *helpmates* have been torn from them, and the hungry cry of helpless babes, were vulgar sorrows that could not move commiseration, though they might extort an alms.

But by far the most notable of the replies to the *Reflections* was Paine's *Rights of Man*, a work published in two parts. The first part, dedicated to George Washington, appeared in March, 1791; the second part, dedicated to Lafayette, appeared about a year later. Although Paine's original intention in writing *Rights of Man* was to answer Burke's *Reflections*, he went far beyond this. In the second part he indicted the British system of government, proposed social reforms, outlined plans for a revolution in England. The social reforms he proposed must have sounded bizarre in 1792. Two centuries later many of these reforms are taken for granted. Paine believed that workingmen had a right to bargain about their wages. He desired free education for the children of the poor; old-age pensions, which should not be regarded as charity but as the interest on taxes that poor working people had paid all their lives; a gift of twenty shillings to each needy woman upon the birth of a child; dowries for married couples; and State lodging houses. Money for these benefits, he suggested, would be raised by a progressive income tax and an inheritance tax.

Such proposals caused less consternation than his attacks on the British government and his plans for overthrowing that government. Faced with possible arrest on the charge of sedition, Paine fled to France.

Burke's *Reflections* sold rapidly — seven thousand copies during the first week after publication, twelve thousand copies within a month. It was soon translated into French, German, and Italian. Reprints in English were distributed in Ireland and America. But the sales of *Rights of Man* were even greater. All over England and in industrial Scotland and Wales workmen chipped in to buy a copy. It achieved its great popularity because its ideas were appealing, the arguments were easy to understand, the style was that of a plain man of the people. Whereas Burke was skilled in turning the kind of phrase that looks impressive when engraved on a monument, Paine used phrases that felt comfortable on the lips of the common man, words that sounded impressive when repeated in taverns and coffeehouses.

Neither Burke nor Paine came off a clear victor in this battle of the books. Burke's understanding of the complexities of government was far greater than Paine's. Burke perceived the dangers of having an established social system destroyed overnight by coffeehouse philosophers. Paine's mind was empty of cultural and political traditions. His judgments of the past were superficial, his hopes for the future too rosy. To Burke must be given the credit for prophesying future events with uncanny accuracy. He anticipated the excesses of the future revolution in France and foresaw a war that would sweep over all Europe. Paine was shortsighted when he inquired loftily, "Who has the National Assembly brought to the scaffold? None!" Within two years after the publication of the *Rights of Man* thousands would have been guillotined. Paine himself barely escaped the guillotine.

Yet Paine did score a point when he charged that Burke was romantically defending the old regime in France while ignoring the sufferings of millions of Frenchmen under the regime. Burke's indignation over the way the mob had treated Marie Antoinette inspired the most famous passage in the *Reflections:*

> I thought ten thousand swords must have leaped from their scabbards to avenge even a look that threatened her with insult. But the age of chivalry is gone. That of sophisters, economists, and calculators has succeeded, and the glory of Europe is extinguished forever.

But that passage is famed primarily for its imagery, not for the depth of the underlying thought. Would the ten thousand swords, had they leapt from their scabbards, have simply defended a queen (a queen, incidentally, whom Burke didn't hold in very high esteem)? Or would they have improved the general welfare of the people of France?

Paine's reply to this was:

> Not one glance of compassion, not one commiserating reflection, that I can find throughout his book, has he bestowed on those who lingered out the most wretched of lives, or life without hope, in the most miserable of prisons . . . He pities the plumage, but forgets the dying bird.

One sentence from the *Reflections* has had unfortunate aftereffects, since it has created the impression that Burke held the common people in great contempt: "Along with its natural protectors and guardians, learning will be cast into the mire, and trodden down under the hoofs of a swinish multitude."

When John Adams read those words, he bristled with indignation and called Burke "an impious reviler of the human species." But Burke was in fact simply paraphrasing Matthew 7:6: "Give not that which is holy unto the dogs, nor cast ye your pearls before swine, lest they trample them under their feet, and turn again and rend you."

Burke, of course, did not measure the effectiveness of the *Reflections* in terms of its sales. He was not, like Paine, trying to appeal to a wide reading audience. *Reflections* was aimed at a sophisticated group of readers, those who could appreciate Burke's arguments. He estimated that no more than four hundred thousand persons in England, Scotland, and Wales (approximately 5 per cent of the total population) possessed the minimum requirements for taking an intelligent interest in public affairs. Even for late eighteenth-century England that estimate was low. The rate of literacy was in fact fairly high at that time. Artisans, domestic servants, and shopkeepers knew how to read and often had free intervals during the day when they could look at newspapers and pamphlets. The newspaper-buying public had increased threefold since the first half of the century. The common man was not necessarily unintelligent simply because he was propertyless, nor was his judgment necessarily uninformed. Burke's respect for the institution of aristocracy is understandable in view of his knowledge of the contributions some aristocrats had made to their country. Paine's respect for the common man arose from his faith in what the common man might accomplish if given an opportunity.

About 1792, when I was entering life, the admiration of the godlike system of the French Revolution was so rife, that only a few old-fashioned Jacobites and the like ventured to hint a preference for the land they lived in, or pretended to doubt that the new principles must be infused into our worn-out constitution. Burke appeared, and all the gibberish about the superior legislation of the French dissolved like an enchanted castle when the destined knight blows his horn before it.

Scott, born in 1771, was young indeed when Burke's *Reflections* was published. Others who changed their minds about the French Revolution and eventually became disciples of Burke were close in age to Scott: William Wordsworth (born 1770), Samuel Taylor Coleridge (born 1772), Robert Southey (born 1774).

It happened that Burke's *Reflections* was published at about the same time as Boswell's *Life of Dr. Johnson*. Fanny Burney recorded in her diary an encounter she had with Boswell one day in October, 1790.

> I stopped him to inquire about Sir Joshua; he said he saw him very often, and that his spirits were very good. I asked about Mr. Burke's book.
>
> "Oh," cried he, "it will come out next week; 'tis the first book in the world, except my own, and that's coming out also very soon; only I want your help."
>
> "My help?"
>
> "Yes, madam; you must give me some of your choice little notes of the Doctor's; we have seen him long enough upon stilts; I want to show him in a new light. Grave Sam, and great Sam, and solemn Sam, and learned Sam — all these he has appeared over and over. Now I want to entwine a wreath of the graces across his brow; I want to show him as gay Sam, agreeable Sam, pleasant Sam; so you must help me with some of his beautiful billets to yourself."

Fanny tried to make an evasive answer. She considered Johnson's letters "sacred" and would never have permitted Boswell to use them. Boswell then said that his *Life of Dr. Johnson* was nearly printed, and pulled a proof sheet out of his pocket to show her. They had now reached the Queen's Lodge, and Boswell evidently expected Fanny to invite him inside. She felt she had no right to do so. Boswell then insisted on reading one of Johnson's letters (from the proof sheet) aloud, giving an excellent imitation of Johnson's manner. A crowd gathered to hear the recital, and Fanny could see that the king and the queen were now approaching. She made a quick apology and darted inside the gate.

Next morning Boswell showed up as she was returning from early prayers at the chapel of St. George. Again he begged for Johnson's letters. Again Fanny refused.

Boswell got his revenge by mentioning her only twice in his biography and then referred to her only briefly. Several months later King George told Fanny that he had looked for her name in the index of the biography and was surprised and disappointed to find so little mention of her. But Fanny wasn't hurt. She was actually relieved that Boswell hadn't said more about her.

Even though Burke and Fox differed in their views of the French Revolution, they remained friends until the spring of 1791. But on April 15 of that year Fox, speaking in the House of Commons, said that the French constitution was the "most stupendous and glorious edifice of liberty which has been created on the foundation of human integrity in any time or country." Burke gasped in indignation while Fox was speaking. He was about to refute Fox's statement when other members called out that they wanted an end to the debate.

But Burke could not be kept silent very long. He started to prepare a speech in reply to Fox's. On May 6 Burke was the first speaker on the subject of a constitution for Canada. This seemed to him an appropriate time to mention the French constitution as an example of what a constitution should not be. Fox and several of his followers shouted that Burke's comments were out of order. (That is, they were not relevant to the subject under debate.) Fox then delivered a speech studded with insulting references to Burke. By the time Fox finished Burke was ready to burst. He rose and started to speak in a restrained tone, which made his hurt and anger only the more evident:

Mr. Fox has ripped up the whole course and tenor of my public and private life, with a considerable degree of asperity. The right honourable gentleman, after having fatigued me with skirmishes of order, which were wonderfully managed by the light infantry of opposition, then brings down upon me the whole strength and heavy artillery of his own judgment, eloquence, and abilities to overwhelm me at once. In carrying on the attack against me, the right honourable gentleman has been supported by a corps of well-disciplined troops, expert in their manouevres and obedient to the word of their commander. I have differed from Mr. Fox in former instances, but no one difference of opinion has ever before for a single moment interrupted our friendship. It certainly is indiscreet at my time of life to provoke enemies, or to give my friends occasion to desert me; yet if a firm and steady adherence to the British constitution places me in such a dilemma, I will risk all; and as public duty and public prudence teach me with my last breath exclaim, ''Fly from the French constitution!''

Fox then realized that he had gone too far. He leaned toward Burke with an agonized whisper: ''There is no loss of friendship.''

''Yes, there is!'' Burke shot back. ''I know the price of my conduct. I have done my duty at the price of my friend. Our friendship is at an end.''

Fox then rose to speak, tears rolling down his cheeks. He begged Burke to remain his friend. Burke refused. They would never be reconciled.

Burke was right in saying it was indiscreet at his time of life to break off friendships. His circle of friends had been narrowing as death took one after another. Now he was losing other friends because he differed with them so intensely over the French Revolution. He had become moody and hard to get along with. Soon he would lose another friend who had been dear to him since youth. Sir Joshua Reynolds died on February 25, 1792.

After Goldsmith's death Burke had become Sir Joshua's closest friend. The two men differed greatly in temperament and may have found each other's company pleasing for that very reason. Reynolds had led an orderly life, marked with high achievement. Burke had achieved much, too, but he had driven himself relentlessly. Reynolds was a calming influence on Burke, but at the same time stimulated him. From Reynolds Burke learned much about the principles and processes of painting and acquired sufficient expertise to be able to detect and foster talent in young artists. And Reynolds learned much from Burke. Burke's concern with aesthetics dated back to his student days, when he wrote the first draft of *Sublime and Beautiful*. He enjoyed discussing aesthetic theories with Reynolds. The artist's *Discourses,* long regarded as important documents in the philosophy of art, undoubtedly owe something to Burke's ideas.

As executor of Sir Joshua's will, Burke took care of the funeral arrangements. The body lay in state at the Royal Academy, and Burke, on behalf of the Reynolds family, made a speech of thanks to the Academicians for the honor they had done to their first president. But his voice became so choked with emotion that he couldn't finish the speech.

Following the services at the Royal Academy, Sir Joshua's body was taken to St. Paul's Cathedral for the last rites. In a letter to young Richard Burke, Burke described the ceremony:

> Everything turned out fortunately for poor Sir Joshua, from the moment of his birth to the hour I saw him laid in the earth. Never was a funeral of ceremony attended with so much sincere concern of all sorts of people. The day was favorable; the order was not broken or interrupted in the smallest degree. Your uncle, who was back in the procession, was struck motionless at his entering at the great west door. The body was just then entering the choir, and the organ began to open, and the long black train before him produced an astonishing effect on his sensibility, on considering how dear to him the object of that melancholy pomp had been. Everything, I think, was just as our deceased friend would, if living, have wished it to be; for

he was, as you know, not altogether indifferent to this kind of observances. He gave, indeed, a direction that no expenses should be employed, but his desire to be buried at St. Paul's Cathedral justified what we have done and all circumstances demanded it.

Sir Joshua's will carried a bequest of 2,000 pounds to Burke and forgave him debts of another 2,000 pounds. The will asked Burke to become guardian of Mary Palmer, Sir Joshua's young niece.

Mary inherited 30,000 pounds from Sir Joshua — a fortune so huge that many eligible bachelors were rumored to be seeking her hand, among them young Richard Burke. But the man whom she actually married — on July 21, 1792 — was Lord Inchiquin, who was sixty-nine at the time. The discrepancy in their ages wasn't as shockingly great as it might have been had she been a young girl. She was forty-one. During the interval between Sir Joshua's death and the wedding Mary lived at Beaconsfield. And for years to come she would be a close friend and neighbor of the Burkes, since Inchiquin's estate was near Beaconsfield.

Among the friends whom Burke lost while he was obsessed with the Hastings trial and the situation in France — but in this case only temporarily — was Fanny Burney. For several years after the opening of the Hastings trial they saw nothing of each other. When, on June 18, 1792, they met at the home of a mutual friend, Fanny was distressed at Burke's apparent coldness. But later in the evening she was overjoyed to learn that because of his poor vision he simply hadn't recognized her. Her diary records:

"Miss Burney!" he now exclaimed, coming forward, and quite kindly taking my hand, "I did not see you," and then he spoke very sweet words of the meeting, and of my looking far better than "while I was a courtier," and of how he rejoiced to see that I so little suited that station. "You look," cried he, "quite renewed, revived, disengaged; you seemed, when I conversed with you last, at the trial, quite altered; I never saw such a change for the better as quitting a Court has brought about."

"Ah!" thought I, this is simply a mistake, from reasoning according to your own feelings. I only seemed altered for the worse at the trial, because I there looked coldly and distantly, from distaste and disaffection to your proceedings, and I have looked changed for the better, only because I here meet you without the chill of disapprobation, and with the flow of my first admiration of you and your talents!

Within a few weeks after this meeting Burke's prophecies in the *Reflections* began to be fulfilled. A Parisian mob stormed the Tuileries on August 10, 1792, slaughtered the Swiss Guard, and took the royal family as prisoners. On January 21, 1793, the revolutionaries guillotined King Louis XVI, thus fulfilling Burke's prediction of their ferocity. Upon learning of this murder, King George sent the French ambassador packing. France then invaded Holland, an ally of Britain. On February 1 the French Convention declared war on England.

20. The Final Years
(1794-1797)

BY THE TIME Burke observed his sixty-fifth birthday, in January, 1794, he had known many seasons of grief. He had outlived many of his dearest friends and closest relatives. But he was not alone. His wife was still living. And his brother Richard and his son Richard. After a strenuous day in Parliament, Burke would return to his London home on Duke Street to find his dear ones gathered at the fireside.

Then, on the night of February 4,1794, his brother Richard came to the Duke Street home for the last time. When he returned to his chambers at Lincoln's Inn that evening, he suffered a severe fit of coughing, from which he did not recover. A few days later he was buried in Saint Mary and All Saints Church in Beaconsfield.

Edmund, as the big brother, had always felt protective toward Richard. When Richard died, Edmund was so overcome with grief that he could hardly carry on his work. But he had to go on with his prosecution of Hastings. Fox and Sheridan might have been entrusted with the responsibility had it not been for Burke's quarrel with them. Now he could trust neither them nor anyone else to carry the fight to the close. And the close of that trial was also the close of Burke's parliamentary career.

From the moment that Burke delivered his first speech in the House of Commons in 1766, he had rubbed King George III the wrong way. At no time had Burke ever tried to curry favor with the king. Yet the king was not blind to Burke's worth. In appreciation for his long parliamentary services, the king now offered him a pension of 2,500 pounds annually, a direct grant from the Crown. The king knew better than to have the pension put to a vote in Parliament. Burke now had few friends in Parliament, and there were many who heartily disliked him. They would have taken a malicious pleasure in slashing the pension to an insulting token sum.

Burke was grateful to the king for the pension. Unlike most other M.P.'s, he was not heir to great wealth. And he had never been paid for his parliamentary services. Besides, he had voted in favor of generous pensions for many other retiring members, even those whose contributions had been far less significant than his own.

After his retirement his greatest satisfaction was knowing that his son Richard, now thirty-six, was about to begin a brilliant parliamentary career. Richard took over his father's seat as representative for the pocket borough of Malton. But immediately after he was elected he became ill. At first the illness aroused no great concern. It was only to be expected as an aftereffect of a boisterous celebration party. But the illness continued. Then the family doctor reported that Richard was suffering from pulmonary tuberculosis, with no hope of recovery. On the morning of August 2, 1794, he died in his father's arms. He was buried beside his uncle Richard in the church at Beaconsfield.

Since birth young Richard had been groomed for a brilliant career. He had received an expensive education, traveled extensively, sat at the table with his father's talented friends. His advantages had been far greater than those that his father had enjoyed at the same age. Now the hopes and dreams of thirty-six years had turned to ashes.

King George offered to elevate Burke to a peerdom, with the title of Lord Beaconsfield. Burke declined the honor, saying, "Those who ought to have succeeded me have gone before." (The title was not used until 1876, when it was bestowed on Prime Minister Benjamin Disraeli, in the year in which he had Queen Victoria proclaimed as Empress of India.)

Burke still had several years to live, but he would never again awake in the morning without a feeling of desolation over his lost son.

A story that circulated about Burke at this time indicated that his grief had driven him out of his mind. According to this story, which was undoubtedly embellished in the retelling, he had been seen running about his fields screaming at the top of his lungs, kissing the horses and cows.

A member of the House of Lords visited Beaconsfield to investigate the story. What had actually happened was something like this: One day while Burke was strolling across one of his fields, an old horse came over to him and nuzzled him. When Burke looked into the mournfully wise eyes of the horse, he was overcome with emotion. That horse had belonged to his son. And it seemed to share his suffering. Burke threw his arms around the horse's neck, kissed its compassionate face, and wept.

No doubt there were other times when memories of his son made him break down temporarily. Yet his accomplishments during his retirement years indicate that his mind was as brilliant as ever.

Beaconsfield had now become a refuge for so many French émigrés that Burke couldn't possibly feed, clothe, and shelter them at his own expense. He begged for gifts and loans from every possible source. With a government subsidy, he established a school at Beaconsfield for the French children.

A touching account of Burke's concern for those children was recorded by Vicomte de Chateaubriand, a young

Frenchman who turned to Burke for help after fleeing from France. "I went to see what he called his 'nursery,' " Chateaubriand reported. "He was amused at the vivacity of the foreign race which was growing up under his paternal genius."

Another account of that school was recorded by James Mackintosh, who had at one time strongly attacked Burke's *Reflections*. Mackintosh changed his mind about that book after visiting France in 1792. He then became friendly with Burke. When Mackintosh visited Beaconsfield late in 1796, he found Burke rolling about on the carpet, laughing and playing with the French children. In conversation with Burke later that day Mackintosh found Burke as "wise and eloquent" as ever and exceedingly well informed about public affairs.

The school was very much on Burke's mind, both during the planning stage, when he was getting the funds to finance it, and later, when he was selecting its staff and supervising its management. It had an enrollment of sixty students, most of them orphans whose parents had perished during the French Revolution. The students wore blue uniforms and hats with white cockades on which were inscribed the words "Vive le Roi." Since most of them came from high-born families, Burke was concerned lest they be disappointed with the simple fare served at the school. (Wealthy eighteenth-century families, in both England and France, were accustomed to enormous, lavish meals.) Sometimes, to make sure the students enjoyed certain delicacies not provided for in the school budget, Burke would "steal" goodies from his family larder. This, according to some visitors at Beaconsfield, would lead to altercations between him and his housekeeper, Mrs. Webster. Mrs. Webster might catch him, for instance, trying to smuggle out a haunch of venison to take over to what she sniffily called "the French people," and a dialogue such as the following might ensue:

MRS. WEBSTER: Sir! I cannot part with my haunch. I cannot indeed. I shall be ruined if I lose my haunch. We shall have nothing else fit to dress for dinner.

BURKE: But, my dear Mrs. Webster, pray consider these poor people. . . .

MRS. WEBSTER: I can consider nothing, Sir, but that we shall have no second course. Give it away to the French people indeed!

BURKE: But those poor people have been accustomed to such things in their own country, and for one day I think we can do without them.

MRS. WEBSTER: Bless me, Sir, remember there are Lord and Lady So-and-So and Mr. and Mrs. So-and-So coming to dinner, and without something of this kind I shall get into shocking disgrace. No, no Sir, I cannot part with my haunch.

Interludes of play with lively children may have done Burke as much good as any medicine. After a visit to the school he would return to the Beaconsfield mansion better able to cope with his many problems. That mansion was now like a hospital, with several invalids demanding attention at the same time. Will Burke had suffered from several strokes and was virtually helpless. Mrs. Jack Nugent, wife of Jane Burke's brother, was seriously ill, as was a more distant kinswoman named Mrs. Burke. Every day Burke observed signs of human misery.

And personal financial troubles still plagued him. On June 30, 1795, he wrote to his friend Walker King:

I send you the letter which I received this morning from the Executors of Lloyd. They will be put off no longer. It is not for me to point out to you the immediate consequences. They are directly upon me. Had I foreseen this, I might perhaps in America, Portugal, or elsewhere, have found a refuge; and the sale of what I have might have gone some way to do justice to my creditors . . . . I cannot quite reconcile my mind to prison with great fortitude.

Because he had been threatened with foreclosure of a mortgage, Burke had started to study Italian, in the belief that he might have to flee the country and end his days in Italy.

It might have have been expected that his enemies would leave him alone now. But there were some who plotted ways of inflicting still more suffering upon him. Late in 1795 the Duke of Bedford and the Earl of Lauderdale, in the House of Lords, launched an attack on Burke for accepting a pension from the king. They charged him with hypocrisy and greed because he had been a strong advocate of economic reform and had severely criticized the royal family for squandering money. Yet he had no scruples about accepting money from the king.

Such a charge from men like Bedford and Lauderdale was a classic example of the pot calling the kettle black. Their families had for generations been grossly opportunistic. Their enormous wealth came from lands that King Henry VIII had granted them, and King Henry VIII had confiscated those lands from the Church and from the older nobility. The current heirs to the property were pampered dandies. They held their seats in the House of Lords because of inherited titles, not because of any personal merits.

If Burke maintained a dignified silence, he would create the impression that the charges against him were true. He decided to answer the charges publicly in "A Letter to a Noble Lord." He said:

> I was not, like his grace of Bedford, swaddled and rocked and dandled into a legislator. *Nitor in adversum* is the motto for a man like me. I possessed not one of the qualities nor cultivated one of the arts that recommend men on the favor and protection of the great. I was not made for a minion or a tool. As little did I follow the trade of winning the hearts by imposing on the understandings of the people. At every step of my progress in life (for in every step I was traversed and opposed) and at every

turnpike I met, I was obliged to show my passport, and again and again to prove my sole title to the honour of being useful to my country, by a proof that I was not wholly unacquainted with its laws and the whole system of its interests both abroad and at home. Otherwise, no rank, no toleration even for me. I had no arts but manly arts. On them I have stood, and, please God, in spite of the Duke of Bedford and the Earl of Lauderdale, to the last gasp will I stand.

Burke denied the charge that he had entered into a bargain when he accepted a pension from the king. He hadn't asked for it. As for the justice of the pension, he considered himself entitled to it, even though he had rendered his services in Parliament without expecting any financial reward. He was elected to Parliament in 1765, the year the Duke of Bedford was born. Yet Bedford, who hadn't troubled himself to make a careful study of Burke's entire parliamentary career, had presumed to pass a sneering judgment on that career. As for accepting a grant directly from the king and without parliamentary consent, that was precisely what the ancestors of Bedford and Lauderdale had done. Burke was an old man with a very young pension. They were young men with very old pensions.

Bedford's assault on Burke was designed partly to win the favor of the French revolutionaries. Burke advised Bedford to consider what could happen to him if British revolutionaries should do what French revolutionaries had done.

I have supported with very great zeal, and I am told with some degree of success, those old prejudices, which buoy up the ponderous mass of his nobility, wealth, and titles. I have omitted no exertion to prevent him and them from sinking to that level, to which the meretricious French faction, his Grace at least coquets with, omit no exertion to reduce both. I have done all I could to discountenance their inquiries into the fortunes of those who hold large portions of wealth without any apparent merit of their own. I have strained every nerve to help the Duke of Bedford in that situation, which alone makes him my superior.

The "Letter to a Noble Lord," despite its defects, is so eloquent that Burke's portrayal of the Duke of Bedford lingers longer in the reader's mind than anything that anyone else might have to say about him. We think of him as stupid, opportunistic, petty. But if we think that, we may be doing him an injustice. Charles James Fox, speaking of Bedford in 1794, had more favorable things to say about him, although Fox, too, was repelled by Bedford's bad manners:

> I look upon him as one of the main pillars of the Party. You know I am one who think both property and rank of great importance in this country with a party view; and, in addition to these, the Duke of Bedford has a very good understanding; I wish I could add popular manners.

Things were going very badly for England as Burke's life neared its end. Several British fleets had mutinied — as he had predicted they might. Napoleon Bonaparte had swept triumphantly through Italy. Spain, now the ally of France, had forced the British navy out of the Mediterranean. And his dear native land was on the brink of revolution.

For several years Burke had been deeply concerned about disquieting reports from Ireland. After the outbreak of the French Revolution he had assumed for a time that the Irish Catholics would serve as "the most effective barrier, the sole barrier against Jacobinism." Instead, as an economically oppressed and politically outlawed group, they were deeply attracted by the French ideals of Liberty, Equality, Fraternity.

Even Burke's old friend Henry Grattan, a fellow-alumnus of Trinity College and former member of the Irish Parliament, seemed to have forsaken his old principles. Grattan had fought for the independence of the Irish Parliament and for Catholic emancipation, causes that Burke supported. But now Grattan had begun to sound as radical as the revolutionary Society of United Irishmen. That society, largely derived from Presbyterian radicalism, aimed at reforming the Irish Parliament, overthrowing the Dublin Castle regime, cutting ties with Great Britain, and establishing a national republic. In 1798 they would precipitate civil war in the country, with the goal of removing all civil and political disabilities deriving from religion and the union of Protestants and Catholics in a secularized democracy, with universal suffrage. Like many religiously tolerant Protestants, Burke felt that most Irish Catholics at that time were unfit to exercise the franchise. He would not have favored universal suffrage for either Catholics or non-Catholics.

One major step he took to curb Jacobinism in Ireland was to help establish a seminary for Irish Catholics at Maynooth. Its purpose was to elevate the intellects of the Irish priests and thus enable them to save Ireland from Jacobinism.

Friends who saw Burke during the final months of his life reported that his attitude toward his approaching death was calm and resigned. He knew he couldn't expect to recover from his bodily infirmities (tuberculous enteritis and possibly cancer), and he didn't care to do anything to prolong his life. But he yielded to the urgings of friends that he go to Bath and partake of its healing waters. He remained in Bath for several months. By the time he returned to Beaconsfield, in May, 1797, he was too weak to hold a pen. Now he had to dictate his letters. And he continued to dictate letters until the last day of his life.

Shortly after midnight on July 9, 1797, he drew his last breath. Charles James Fox had begged to be allowed to visit him during his final weeks, but Burke had refused to be reconciled.

Jane Burke sent a note to Fox, written in the third person and therefore a bit cooler than a letter in the first person might have been. Yet there is no bitterness in its tone:

Mrs. Burke presents her compliments to Mr. Fox and thanks him for his obliging inquiries. Mrs. Burke communicated his letter to Mr. Burke, and, by his desire, has to inform Mr. Fox that it has cost Mr. Burke the most heartfelt pain to obey the stern voice of his duty in rending asunder a long friendship, but he deemed this sacrifice necessary, that his principles remained the same, and that in whatever of life yet remained to him, he conceives he must live for others and not for himself. Mr. Burke is convinced that the principles which he has endeavoured to maintain are necessary to the welfare and dignity of his country, and that these principles can be enforced only by the general persuasion of his sincerity. For herself, Mrs. Burke has again to express her gratitude to Mr. Fox for his inquiries.

Burke's attitude toward Fox may seem to be coldly unforgiving. But there was probably more to it than that. Especially during his final days, Burke may well have felt that the sight of Fox's face would be intolerably painful. The affection that Burke had once felt for Fox was never completely extinguished. In a conversation with James Mackintosh late in 1796 Burke said of Fox, "He is made to be loved."

At news of Burke's death Fox proposed, in the House of Commons, that Burke be honored with a public funeral and burial in Westminster Abbey. But that was precisely the kind of funeral that Burke did not wish. He had left instructions for a simple private funeral.

Burke feared that the Jacobins (the group largely responsible for the atrocities of the French Revolution) might one day invade England. And if they did, they might exhume and dishonor his body. He therefore asked that his body be placed in a lead coffin and buried in a secret place. Such fears could be interpreted as paranoid. But Burke was certainly not irrational in believing that he had enemies. His attacks on the Jacobins had given them good cause to hate him.

The funeral, held at the Beaconsfield church on July 15, was attended only by relatives, a few close friends, and some Beaconsfield neighbors.

Among the mourners was Fanny Burney — now Mme. Alexandre-Jean-Baptiste Piochard d'Arblay, wife of an expatriate French military officer. Shortly after the funeral she wrote to her father:

> How sincerely I sympathize in all you say of that truly great man! That his enemies say he was not perfect is nothing compared with his immense superiority over almost all those who are merely exempted from his peculiar defects. That he was upright in heart, even where he acted wrong, I do truly believe... and that he asserted nothing he had not persuaded himself to be true, from Mr. Hastings's being the most rapacious of villains, to the King's being incurably insane. He was as generous as kind, and as liberal in his sentiments as he was luminous in intellect and extraordinary in abilities and eloquence. Though free from all little vanity, high above envy, and glowing with zeal to exalt talents and merit in others, he had, I believe, a consciousness of his own greatness, that shut out those occasional and useful self-doubts which keep our judgment in order, by calling our actions and our passions to account.

Jane Burke survived her husband by fifteen years. And during those years her constant companion was Burke's niece, Mary French Haviland. Mary's husband, a Captain Haviland, had died of a fever in Martinique shortly before their son was born in 1795.

The son, whose name was Thomas William Aston Haviland, was the last male representative of Edmund Burke's family (although he was, of course, not a direct descendant of Edmund). He was called to the bar in 1823, but never practiced law. He changed his last name to Haviland-Burke, in homage to his great-uncle, and devoted his life to acts of public benevolence and the cultivation of the fine arts.

In 1811, a year before her death, Jane sold Beaconsfield to a neighbor, James Du Pre, for 38,500 pounds, with the provision that she be allowed the use of the house and grounds for as long as she lived. With the proceeds from that sale, she was able to make provision in her will for the repayment of all her husband's debts, as well as the debts of the two Richards, his brother and his son. She died on April 2, 1812, at the age of seventy-eight.

It is sad that no Burke descendant ever bore the stately title of Lord Beaconsfield. Yet Burke's true descendants are to be found, not on genealogical charts but in the catalogues of great libraries. More and more entries are added each year under the heading "Burke, Edmund, 1729-1797." Burke himself wrote millions upon millions of words. Even more millions of words have been written by those who have drawn inspiration from his ideas or who have tried to interpret those ideas to later generations. Interpretations may vary according to the background and bias of the writer. But so long as libraries continue to exist, Edmund Burke's name will live on.

Postscript

"None knew better than Burke how thin is the lava layer between the costly fabric of society and the volcanic heats and destroying flames of anarchy."

When I came across that sentence, very early in my research for this biography, I drew a pencil line beside it. I understood, or thought I understood, that sentence even on first reading. I liked it for the beauty of its imagery as much as for its meaning. Maybe, I thought, I'd use it somewhere in the text. I didn't. One comes across many good things while doing research for a biography, and some of those good things must remain in the notes.

Several years after I read that sentence for the first time, I read it again. This time it took on a radiance that I hadn't originally perceived. It became something more than a significant idea expressed in poetic language. When I tried to explain it to someone else, I found that I had to use more prosaic language. "The costly fabric of society" refers to the benefits that civilization has passed on to us over the centuries. And the words "the volcanic heats and destroying flames of anarchy" refer to those drastic, ill-considered social changes that may destroy most of the benefits of civilization. The lava layer is that thin — but, oh so significant! — filling between these two layers.

That sentence is worth pondering after one has heard the story of Burke's life. It explains so much about him. And it helps to link him with our own times.

For we live in a world where the lava layer is even thinner than it was in Burke's day. We've been living in that world ever since that August day in 1945 when an atom bomb fell on Hiroshima.

The man who wrote the sentence I have quoted never knew about the atom bomb. He was Augustine Birrell, a liberal Member of Parliament during the late nineteenth and early twentieth century.

If Burke is known today as a great conservative, it is because he cared so much about preserving the "costly fabric of society," even though he was well aware of its imperfections. The causes he supported were similar to the causes that might be supported by today's liberals. But we could hardly expect them to be precisely the same causes. Burke should be judged by the standards of his own times.

From boyhood Burke knew how ruthless the powerful can be in crushing the powerless. Growing up in eighteenth-century Ireland in a half-Catholic, half-Protestant family is a good way to acquire such knowledge. The boy who wept at the sight of an Irish tenant being evicted would become the man who devoted his long parliamentary career to fighting for the civil rights of all British subjects.

Civil rights! To those who live in twentieth-century America those words call up an image of affluent white suburbanites linking arms with ghetto blacks and chanting "We shall overcome." But Burke was fighting for civil rights even before the American colonies broke away from the mother country. And he was well aware that civil rights acquired by Britons over the centuries could be rapidly wiped out if a great break should occur in the thin lava layer that shielded civilization from anarchy.

Burke died believing that such a great break would soon occur. Before Napoleon was born, Burke had started to fight in the House of Commons for the rights of the American colonies. By the time Burke died, in 1797, Napoleon had begun his conquest of Europe. As Burke neared death, he believed that a foreign host might soon invade England.

He didn't care to have any monuments erected in his honor. But he did use the word "monument" in a figurative sense in a letter written during the last year of his life. There he stated that his only "monument" would be the work he had done in exposing political corruption in India. "Let my endeavours to save the Nation from that shame and guilt be my monument; the only one I ever will have."

It was not the only monument he would ever have, in either the figurative or the literal sense. His ideas about how nations should be governed live on, although they are more likely to be studied today by graduate students seeking doctorates than by politicians seeking public office. And statues in his honor have been erected in his native Ireland and in England.

There's a statue of Burke in Washington, D.C., too. It stands in a tiny triangular park at the intersection of 11th and L Streets and Massachusetts Avenue. Not long ago I pointed it out to a cab driver as we were passing that park. To my amazement — for the cab driver had been grumpily sounding off on what a mess the world was in — he suddenly changed his tone and, in a fine oratorical voice, quoted a few words from Burke. Words memorized in long ago schooldays, now dredged up in reply to a passenger he would never see again once we'd parted company at the Union Station.

That station had recently been beautified for our bicentennial celebration. To me, as perhaps to many others, the sight of so many patriotic symbols brings a rush of schoolday memories. Singing patriotic songs, reciting patriotic poems. Pledging allegiance to the flag of the United States of America and to the republic for which it stands. To me, as a native of the Bay State, it also brings back memories of field trips to Boston. Two spinster schoolmarms guided us, the children of immigrants, along the route that would in time be known as "The Freedom Trail." And once, singing patriotic songs all the way, we took a bus out to Concord to view the place where a minuteman's musket fired the shot heard round the world.

Today a ballistic missile launched six thousand miles away could, within minutes, destroy all the magnificent monuments in Washington. But the destruction of those monuments would be far less tragic than the destruction of the ideals they symbolize.

Burke's monument in Washington attracts little attention. My cab driver probably drove past that monument several times a day for many years without ever noticing it — until I called it to his attention. But I like to think that he now points it out to some of his passengers. For Burke, who never set foot on American soil, was as great an American patriot as some who have been memorialized by grander monuments.

A.P.M.

BIBLIOGRAPHY

Aldridge, Alfred Owen. *Man of Reason: The Life of Thomas Paine.* Philadelphia: Lippincott, 1959.

Ayling, Stanley. *George the Third.* New York: Alfred A. Knopf, 1976.

Bailyn, Bernard. *The Ideological Origins of the American Revolution.* Cambridge, Mass.: The Belknap Press of Harvard University Press, 1962.

Bate, W. Jackson. *Samuel Johnson.* New York and London: Harcourt Brace Jovanovich, 1977.

Brinton, Crane. *A Decade of Revolution, 1789–1799.* New York: Harper & Bros., 1934.

British Medical Association. *Porphyria – A Royal Malady.* London: British Medical Asso., 1968.

Brooks, John. *King George III: A Biography of America's Last Monarch.* New York: McGraw-Hill, 1972.

Brown, Philip Anthony. *The French Revolution in English History.* New York: Barnes and Noble, 1918, 3rd printing, 1965.

Bryant, Donald Cross. *Edmund Burke and His Literary Friends.* St. Louis: Washington University Studies, New Series, No. 9, 1939.

Burton, Elizabeth. *The Pageant of Georgian England.* New York: Charles Scribner's Sons, 1967.

Chapman, Gerald. *Edmund Burke: The Practical Imagination.* Cambridge, Mass.: Harvard University Press, 1967.

Charles-Edwards, T., and Richardson, E. *They Saw It Happen: An Anthology of Eyewitness Accounts of Events in British History, 1689–1827.* New York: Macmillan, 1955.

Churchill, Winston. *A History of the English-Speaking Peoples,* Vol. III, *The Age of Revolution.* New York: Dodd, Mead, 1965.

Clarke, John. *The Life and Times of George III.* London: Weidenfeld & Nicolson, 1972.

Clive, John. *Macaulay: The Shaping of the Historian.* New York: Alfred A. Knopf, 1973.

Cobban, Alfred, and Smith, Robert A., eds. *The Correspondence of Edmund Burke*, Vol. VI, *July 1789–Dec. 1791*. Chicago: University of Chicago Press, 1967.

Cobban, Alfred. *Edmund Burke and the Revolt against the Eighteenth Century: A Study of the Political and Social Thinking of Burke, Wordsworth, Coleridge, and Southey*. New York: Macmillan, 1929.

Cone, Carl B. *Burke and the Nature of Politics*, Vol. I, *The Age of the American Revolution*. Louisville, Ky: University of Kentucky Press, 1957.

———. *Burke and the Nature of Politics*, Vol. II, *The Age of the French Revolution*. Louisville, Ky.: University of Kentucky Press, 1964.

Cook, Alfred S., ed. *Edmund Burke's Speech on Conciliation with America*. New York: Longmans, Green & Co., 1905.

Cook, Fred J. *Dawn over Saratoga: The Turning Point of the Revolutionary War*. Garden City, N. Y.: Doubleday, 1973.

Coolidge, Olivia. *Tom Paine, Revolutionary*. New York: Charles Scribner's Sons, 1969.

Copeland, Thomas W. *Our Eminent Friend Edmund Burke: Six Essays*. New Haven, Conn.: Yale University Press, 1949.

———, ed. *The Correspondence of Edmund Burke*, Vol. I, *April 1744–June 1768*. Chicago: University of Chicago Press, 1958.

Coupland, Sir Reginald. *The American Revolution and the British Empire*, The Sir George Watson Lectures for 1928 at the University of London, 1928-1929. London: Longmans, Green, 1930.

Creasey, John. *The Masters of Bow Street*. New York: Simon & Schuster, 1974.

Daiches, David. *James Boswell and His World*. New York: Charles Scribner's Sons, 1976.

Davidson, Marshall B. and the Editors of *Horizon*. *The Horizon History of the World in 1776*. New York: American Heritage, 1975.

Davis, David Brion. *The Problem of Slavery in the Age of the Revolution*. Ithaca, N.Y.: Cornell University Press, 1975.

Derry, John W. *Charles James Fox*. New York: St. Martin's Press, 1972.

Dupuy, Colonels R. Ernest and Trevor N. *The Compact History of the Revolutionary War*. New York: Hawthorn, 1963.

Ebenstein, William. *Great Political Thinkers, Plato to the Present*, 4th ed. New York: Holt, Rinehart and Winston. 1969.

Ehrman, John. *The Younger Pitt: The Years of Acclaim*. New York: E. P. Dutton, 1960.

Eyck, Erich. *Pitt* vs. *Fox, Father and Son, 1735–1806*. London: G. Bell & Sons, 1950.

Feiling, Keith, *Warren Hastings*. London: Macmillan, 1954.

Flexner, Eleanor. *Mary Wollstonecraft: A Biography*. New York: Coward, McCann, and Geoghegan, 1972.

Freeman, William. *Oliver Goldsmith*. New York: Philosophical Library, 1952.

Furber, Holden, ed. *Correspondence of Edmund Burke*, Vol. V. *July 1782–June 1789*. Chicago: University of Chicago Press, 1965.

Gibbs, Lewis, ed. *The Diary of Fanny Burney*. London: J.M. Dent & Sons, 1940.

Graubard, Stephen Richards. *Burke, Disraeli and Churchill: The Politics of Perseverance*. Cambridge, Mass.: Harvard University Press, 1961.

Green, Walford Davis, M. P. *William Pitt, Earl of Chatham and the Growth and Division of the British Empire, 1707-1778*. London: G. P. Putnam's Sons, 1961.

Guttridge, George H., ed. *The Correspondence of Edmund Burke*, Vol. III, *July 1774–June 1775*. Chicago: University of Chicago Press, 1961.

Halliday, F. E. *Doctor Johnson and His World*. New York: Viking, 1968.

Henlow, Joyce. *The History of Fanny Burney*. Oxford: Clarendon Press, 1958.

Hibbert, Christopher. *London: The Biography of a City*. New York: William Morrow, 1969.

———. *The Personal History of Samuel Johnson*. New York: Harper & Row, 1971.

Hobhouse, Christopher. *Fox*. London: John Murray, 1934.

Hodgart, Matthew, ed. *Horace Walpole, Memoirs and Portraits*. New York: Macmillan, 1963.

Hoffman, Ross J. S., and Levack, Paul. *Burke's Politics: Selected Writings and Speeches of Edmund Burke on Reform, Revolution and War*. New York: Alfred A. Knopf, 1948.

Hudleston, F. J. *Gentleman Johnny Burgoyne*. Indianapolis: Bobbs-Merrill, 1927.

Hudson, Derek. *Sir Joshua Reynolds: A Personal Study*. London: Geoffrey Blas, 1956.

Hyde, Mary. *The Impossible Friendship: Boswell and Mrs. Thrale*. Cambridge, Mass.: Harvard University Press, 1972.

Kirk, Russell. *A Program for Conservatives*. Chicago: Henry Regnery, 1954.

———. *Edmund Burke: A Genius Reconsidered*. New York: Arlington House, 1967.

Kramnick, Isaac. *Edmund Burke: Great Lives Observed*. Englewood Cliffs, N.J.: Prentice-Hall, 1967.

———. *The Rage of Edmund Burke: Portrait of an Ambivalent Conservative*. New York: Basic Books, 1977.

Laski, Harold J. *Political Thought in England from Locke to Bentham*. London: Home University Library, 1944.

Laver, James. *The Age of Illusion: Manners and Morals, 1750-1848*. New York: David McKay, 1972.

Lloyd, Alan. *The King Who Lost America: A Portrait of the Life and Times of George III*. New York: Doubleday, 1971.

Long, J. S. *George III: The Story of a Complex Man*. Boston: Little, Brown, 1960.

Lucas, F. L. *Search for Good Sense: Four Eighteenth-Century Characters: Johnson, Chesterfield, Boswell, Goldsmith*. New York: Macmillan, 1958.

———. *Art of Living: Four Eighteenth-Century Minds: Hume, Horace Walpole, Burke, Benjamin Franklin*. New York: Macmillan, 1959.

Magnus, Sir Philip. *Edmund Burke, A Life*. London: John Murray, 1939.

Mahoney, Thomas H. D. *Edmund Burke and Ireland*. Cambridge, Mass.: Harvard University Press, 1960.

Maier, Pauline. *From Resistance to Revolution: Colonial Radicals and the Development of American Opposition to Britain, 1765-1776*. New York: Alfred A. Knopf, 1972.

Marshall, Dorothy. *Eighteenth-Century England*. New York: David McKay, 1962.

Marshall, R.J., and Woods, John A., eds. *The Correspondence of Edmund Burke*, Vol. VII, *January 1792-August 1794*. Chicago: University of Chicago Press, 1968.

Maxwell, Constantia. *A History of Trinity College, Dublin, 1596-1892*. Dublin: The University Press, Trinity College, 1946.

McDowell, R.B., ed. *The Correspondence of Edmund Burke*, Vol. VIII, *September 1794-April 1796*. Chicago: University of Chicago Press, 1969.

———— and Woods, John A., eds. *The Correspondence of Edmund Burke*, Vol. IX, *May 1796-July 1797*. Chicago: University of Chicago Press, 1970.

Miller, John C. *Origins of the American Revolution*. Stanford, Calif.: Stanford University Press, 1959.

Morgan, Edmund S. and Helen M. *The Stamp Act Crisis: Prologue to Revolution*. Chapel Hill, N.C.: University of North Carolina Press, 1953.

Morison, Samuel Eliot. *The Oxford History of the American People*. New York: Oxford University Press, 1965.

Morris, Charles H., ed. *Burke's Speech on Conciliation with America, and Edmund Burke, an Essay, by Augustine Birrell*. New York: Harper & Bros., 1945.

Morris, Richard S. *The Peacemakers: The Great Powers and American Independence*. New York: Harper & Row, 1965.

Namier, Lewis B. *England in the Age of the American Revolution*, 2nd ed. London: Macmillan, 1966.

Newman, Bertram. *Edmund Burke*. Freeport, N.Y.: Books for Libraries Press, 1959. (1st ed., 1927)

Pearson, Hesketh. *Johnson and Boswell: The Story of Their Lives*. New York: Harper & Bros., 1958.

Pearson, Michael. *Those Damned Rebels: The American Revolution as Seen through British Eyes*. New York: G. P. Putnam's Sons, 1972.

Quennell, Peter. *Samuel Johnson: His Friends and Enemies*. New York: American Heritage Press, 1972.

Ritcheson, Charles R. *British Politics and the American Revolution*. Norman, Okla.: University of Oklahoma Press, 1954.

Rudé, George. *Hanoverian London, 1714-1808*. Berkeley: University of California Press, 1971.

Ryskamp, Charles and Pottle, Frederick A., eds. *Boswell: The Ominous Years 1774-1775*. New York: McGraw-Hill, 1963.

Samuels, Arthur P. J. *Early Life, Correspondence, and Writings of the Rt. Hon. Edmund Burke with a Transcript of the Minute Book of the Debating Club founded by him in Trinity College, Dublin*. Cambridge, England: Cambridge University Press, 1923.

Schlesinger, Arthur M., with an introduction by Schlesinger, Arthur M., Jr. *The Birth of a Nation: A Portrait of the American People on the Eve of Independence*. New York: Alfred A. Knopf. 1969.

Sherwin, Oscar. *Goldy: The Life and Times of Oliver Goldsmith*. New York: Twayne Publishers, 1961.

Spear, Percival. *India: A Modern History*. Ann Arbor, Mich.: University of Michigan Press, 1961.

Stanlis, Peter J., et al. *Edmund Burke: Enlightenment in the Modern World*. Detroit: University of Detroit Press, 1967.

Stephen, Leslie. *English Literature and Society in the Eighteenth Century*. London: Gerald Duckworth, 1906.

Sutherland, Lucy S., ed. *The Correspondence of Edmund Burke*, Vol. II, *July 1768–June 1774*. Chicago: University of Chicago Press, 1960.

Trevelyan, G. M. *English Social History: A Survey of Six Centuries, Chaucer to Queen Victoria*. London: Longmans, Green, 1942.

Turberville, A. S. *The House of Lords in the XVIIIth Century*. Oxford, England: Clarendon Press, 1927.

Wain, John. *Samuel Johnson: A Biography*. New York: Viking, 1974.

Ward, Sir A.W., and Waller, A.B. *The Cambridge History of English Literature*, Vol. XI: *The Period of the French Revolution*. Cambridge, England: Cambridge University Press, 1953.

White, R. J. *The Age of George III*. New York: Walker & Co., 1968.

Wickwire, Franklin and Mary. *Cornwallis: The American Adventure*. Boston: Houghton Mifflin, 1970.

Williams, Basil. *The Life of William Pitt, Earl of Chatham*, Vol. II. London: Longmans, Green, 1915.

Woods, John A., ed. *Correspondence of Edmund Burke*, Vol. IV, *July 1778–June 1782*. Chicago: University of Chicago Press, 1963.

INDEX

List of Illustrations

Dr. Samuel Johnson. From portrait by John Opie in the National Galleries of Scotland. Reproduced from photograph, National Portrait Gallery.

Oliver Goldsmith. From a portrait by Reynolds, National Portrait Gallery.

Sir Joshua Reynolds. Self-portrait as President of the Royal Academy of Arts, Royal Academy of Arts, London.

James Boswell. From portrait by Reynolds, National Portrait Gallery.

Warren Hastings. From painting by Sir Thomas Lawrence, 1811, National Portrait Gallery.

About the Author

Alice P. Miller holds graduate degrees in sociology and psychology from the New School for Social Research and Columbia University and has taught those subjects at Pratt Institute and the Juilliard School of Music. Several of her books for juveniles have won Indiana University awards and been selected by the Scholastic book clubs. In 1976, while researching her biography of Edmund Burke, she won an award in the Woman's Day Bicentennial Essay contest. She resides in New York with her husband.